LANGUAGE AND LITERACY

Dorothy S. Strickland, FOUN...

Celia Genishi and Donna E. Alverm...

W9-BWR-317

ADVISORY BOARD: Richard Allington, Kathryn Au, Bernice Cull... ...Haas Dyson,
Carole Edelsky, Shirley Brice Heath, Connie Juel, Susan Lytle, Timothy Shanahan

Overtested: How High-Stakes Accountability Fails
English Language Learners
JESSICA ZACHER PANDYA

Restructuring Schools for Linguistic Diversity:
Linking Decision Making to Effective Programs,
Second Edition
OFELIA B. MIRAMONTES, ADEL NADEAU,
& NANCY L. COMMINS

Words Were All We Had:
Becoming Biliterate Against the Odds
MARÍA DE LA LUZ REYES, ED.

Urban Literacies: Critical Perspectives on Language,
Learning, and Community
VALERIE KINLOCH, ED.

Bedtime Stories and Book Reports:
Connecting Parent Involvement and Family Literacy
CATHERINE COMPTON-LILLY & STUART GREENE, EDS.

Envisioning Knowledge: Building Literacy in the
Academic Disciplines
JUDITH A. LANGER

Envisioning Literature: Literary Understanding and
Literature Instruction, Second Edition
JUDITH A. LANGER

Writing Assessment and the Revolution in Digital
Texts and Technologies
MICHAEL R. NEAL

Artifactual Literacies: Every Object Tells a Story
KATE PAHL & JENNIFER ROWSELL

Educating Emergent Bilinguals: Policies, Programs,
and Practices for English Language Learners
OFELIA GARCÍA & JO ANNE KLEIFGEN

(Re)Imagining Content-Area Literacy Instruction
RONI JO DRAPER, ED.

Change Is Gonna Come: Transforming Literacy
Education for African American Students
PATRICIA A. EDWARDS, GWENDOLYN THOMPSON MCMILLON, &
JENNIFER D. TURNER

When Commas Meet Kryptonite: Classroom Lessons
from the Comic Book Project
MICHAEL BITZ

Literacy Tools in the Classroom: Teaching Through
Critical Inquiry, Grades 5–12
RICHARD BEACH, GERALD CAMPANO, BRIAN EDMISTON,
& MELISSA BORGMANN

Harlem on Our Minds: Place, Race, and the Literacies
of Urban Youth
VALERIE KINLOCH

Teaching the New Writing: Technology, Change, and
Assessment in the 21st-Century Classroom
ANNE HERRINGTON, KEVIN HODGSON, & CHARLES MORAN, EDS.

Critical Encounters in High School English: Teaching
Literary Theory to Adolescents, Second Edition
DEBORAH APPLEMAN

Children, Language, and Literacy: Diverse Learners in
Diverse Times
CELIA GENISHI & ANNE HAAS DYSON

Children's Language: Connecting Reading, Writing,
and Talk
JUDITH WELLS LINDFORS

The Administration and Supervision of Reading
Programs, Fourth Edition
SHELLEY B. WEPNER & DOROTHY S. STRICKLAND, EDS.

"You Gotta BE the Book": Teaching Engaged and
Reflective Reading with Adolescents, Second Edition
JEFFREY D. WILHELM

No Quick Fix: Rethinking Literacy Programs in
America's Elementary Schools, The RTI Reissue
RICHARD L. ALLINGTON & SEAN A. WALMSLEY, EDS.

Children's Literature and Learning: Literary Study
Across the Curriculum
BARBARA A. LEHMAN

Storytime: Young Children's Literary Understanding in
the Classroom
LARWRENCE R. SIPE

Effective Instruction for Struggling Readers, K–6
BARBARA M. TAYLOR & JAMES E. YSSELDYKE, EDS.

The Effective Literacy Coach: Using Inquiry to Support
Teaching and Learning
ADRIAN RODGERS & EMILY M. RODGERS

Writing in Rhythm: Spoken Word Poetry in Urban
Classrooms
MAISHA T. FISHER

Reading the Media: Media Literacy in High School English
RENEE HOBBS

teaching**media**_literacy_.com: A Web-Linked Guide to
Resources and Activities
RICHARD BEACH

What Was It Like? Teaching History and Culture
Through Young Adult Literature
LINDA J. RICE

Once Upon a Fact: Helping Children Write Nonfiction
CAROL BRENNAN JENKINS & ALICE EARLE

Research on Composition: Multiple Perspectives on
Two Decades of Change
PETER SMAGORINSKY, ED.

Critical Literacy/Critical Teaching: Tools for Preparing
Responsive Literacy Teachers
CHERYL DOZIER, PETER JOHNSTON, & REBECCA ROGERS

The Vocabulary Book: Learning and Instruction
MICHAEL F. GRAVES

Building on Strength: Language and Literacy in Latino
Families and Communities
ANA CELIA ZENTELLA, ED.

Powerful Magic: Learning from Children's Responses
to Fantasy Literature
NINA MIKKELSEN

(Continued)

For volumes in the NCRLL Collection (edited by JoBeth Allen and Donna E. Alvermann) and the Practitioners Bookshelf Series
(edited by Celia Genishi and Donna E. Alvermann), please visit www.tcpress.com.

LANGUAGE AND LITERACY SERIES (*continued*)

New Literacies in Action:
Teaching and Learning in Multiple Media
WILLIAM KIST

Teaching English Today: Advocating Change in the
Secondary Curriculum
BARRIE R.C. BARRELL, ROBERTA F. HAMMETT,
JOHN S. MAYHER, & GORDON M. PRADL, EDS.

Bridging the Literacy Achievement Gap, 4–12
DOROTHY S. STRICKLAND & DONNA E. ALVERMANN, EDS.

Crossing the Digital Divide: Race, Writing, and
Technology in the Classroom
BARBARA MONROE

Out of This World: Why Literature Matters to Girls
HOLLY VIRGINIA BLACKFORD

Critical Passages: Teaching the Transition to College
Composition
KRISTIN DOMBEK & SCOTT HERNDON

Making Race Visible:
Literary Research for Cultural Understanding
STUART GREENE & DAWN ABT-PERKINS, EDS.

The Child as Critic: Developing Literacy Through
Literature, K–8, Fourth Edition
GLENNA SLOAN

Room for Talk: Teaching and Learning in a
Multilingual Kindergarten
REBEKAH FASSLER

Give Them Poetry! A Guide for Sharing Poetry with
Children K–8
GLENNA SLOAN

The Brothers and Sisters Learn to Write
ANNE HAAS DYSON

"Just Playing the Part"
CHRISTOPHER WORTHMAN

The Testing Trap
GEORGE HILLOCKS, JR.

School's Out!
GLYNDA HULL & KATHERINE SCHULTZ, EDS.

Reading Lives
DEBORAH HICKS

Inquiry Into Meaning
EDWARD CHITTENDEN & TERRY SALINGER, WITH ANNE M. BUSSIS

"Why Don't They Learn English?"
LUCY TSE

Conversational Borderlands
BETSY RYMES

Inquiry-Based English Instruction
RICHARD BEACH & JAMIE MYERS

The Best for Our Children
MARÍA DE LA LUZ REYES & JOHN J. HALCÓN, EDS.

Language Crossings
KAREN L. OGULNICK, ED.

What Counts as Literacy?
MARGARET GALLEGO & SANDRA HOLLINGSWORTH, EDS.

Beginning Reading and Writing
DOROTHY S. STRICKLAND & LESLEY M. MORROW, EDS.

Reading for Meaning
BARBARA M. TAYLOR, MICHAEL F. GRAVES,
& PAUL VAN DEN BROEK, EDS.

Young Adult Literature and the New Literary Theories
ANNA O. SOTER

Literacy Matters
ROBERT P. YAGELSKI

Children's Inquiry
JUDITH WELLS LINDFORS

Close to Home
JUAN C. GUERRA

On the Brink
SUSAN HYNDS

Life at the Margins
JULIET MERRIFIELD, ET AL.

Literacy for Life
HANNA ARLENE FINGERET & CASSANDRA DRENNON

The Book Club Connection
SUSAN I. MCMAHON & TAFFY E. RAPHAEL, EDS., WITH VIRGINIA
J. GOATLEY & LAURA S. PARDO

Until We Are Strong Together
CAROLINE E. HELLER

Writing Superheroes
ANNE HAAS DYSON

Opening Dialogue
MARTIN NYSTRAND, ET AL.

Just Girls
MARGARET J. FINDERS

The First R
MICHAEL F. GRAVES, PAUL VAN DEN BROEK, &
BARBARA M. TAYLOR, EDS.

Teaching Writing as Reflective Practice
GEORGE HILLOCKS, JR.

Talking Their Way into Science
KAREN GALLAS

The Languages of Learning
KAREN GALLAS

Partners in Learning
CAROL LYONS, GAY SU PINNELL, & DIANE DEFORD

Social Worlds of Children Learning to Write in an
Urban Primary School
ANNE HAAS DYSON

Inside/Outside
MARILYN COCHRAN-SMITH & SUSAN L. LYTLE

Whole Language Plus
COURTNEY B. CAZDEN

Learning to Read
G. BRIAN THOMPSON & TOM NICHOLSON, EDS.

Engaged Reading
JOHN T. GUTHRIE & DONNA E. ALVERMANN

OVERTESTED

How High-Stakes Accountability
Fails English Language Learners

Jessica Zacher Pandya

Foreword by Robert Rueda

Teachers College, Columbia University
New York and London

KH

Published by Teachers College Press, 1234 Amsterdam Avenue, New York, NY 10027

Library of Congress Cataloging-in-Publication Data

Pandya, Jessica Zacher.
  Overtested : How high-stakes accountability fails English language learners / Jessica Zacher Pandya ; foreword by Robert Rueda.
    p. cm. — (Language and literacy series)
  Includes bibliographical references and index.
  ISBN 978-0-8077-5247-0 (pbk. : alk. paper)
  ISBN 978-0-8077-5248-7 (hardcover : alk. paper)
  1. English language—Study and teaching—Foreign speakers. 2. Language and languages—Study and teaching. 3. English language—Ability testing. 4. Education—Social aspects—United States. 5. Critical pedagogy—United States. I. Title.
PE1128.A2P287 2011
428.0076—dc23   2011017772

ISBN 978-0-8077-5247-0 (paper)
ISBN 978-0-8077-5248-7 (hardcover)

Printed on acid-free paper
Manufactured in the United States of America

18 17 16 15 14 13 12 11   8 7 6 5 4 3 2 1

11/26/12

To my children, Isabella and Valmik

Contents

Foreword by Robert Rueda ix

Preface xi

Acknowledgments xiii

1. **When Testing and Language
   Learning Are Synonymous** 1
   Introducing the California Context 4
   In Ms. Romano's Classroom:
   Setting Goals for and with English Language Learners 7
   Organization of the Book 11

2. **High-Volume, High-Stakes
   Testing in Elementary Schools** 13
   Accountability and Surveillance
   in the Elementary Classroom 14
   Sorting Out the Effects of Standardized Tests 17
   A Classroom Conversation About Testing 24
   Consequences and Solutions:
   What Is Wrong and How to Fix It 26

3. **Using Mandated, Structured
   Curricula with English Language Learners** 31
   The Lure of Science and Success 31
   Opposition to Structured Curricula 34
   Instructional Practices and Literacy Events
   in the Structured Curriculum Classroom 37
   Consequences of Using Structured Curricula 56

Limited Time and Available
Meaningful Opportunities for ELD   57

Implications: What to Keep,
What to Remove, What to Substitute   58

4. **Grappling with the Complexities
   of a Classroom of English Language Learners**   **61**

   From Beginner to English Only,
   and Everything in Between   62

   Overarching Issues and Recommendations:
   How to Help English Language Learners   73

5. **Learning to Teach in the Age of Accountability**   **79**

   Preparing Teacher Candidates to
   Teach ELLs in the Age of Accountability   80

   Assessing Teacher Candidates   82

   Teaching in a Value-Added World   86

   Educating and Supporting Teachers
   of ELLs in High-Stakes Settings   91

   Contextualizing Teacher Education in
   the Age of Accountability   94

6. **Policy and Practice Changes
   in Assessment and Instruction**   **96**

   One Standardized, Large-Scale
   Content-Area Test Per Educational Level   96

   Policy Changes in the Assessment of
   English Language Learners   100

   Policy and Content Changes for Teacher
   Education Regarding English Language Learners   103

   In Closing: Learning in the Age of Accountability   105

Notes   **107**

References   **111**

Index   **131**

About the Author   **143**

Foreword

When I started my career over 2 decades ago, there was not much work on the group of students who are now called English learners. I began looking into the educational issues of students who were not native English speakers in the course of completing my doctoral coursework at a major research university. I recall that, at the time, the only faculty member who was actively doing research in this area was focusing on how bilingualism interferes with "correct" English speech. The work started from the premise that the second language was a negative influence and proceeded to focus on a search for language deficits. Fortunately, research on English learners and bilingualism has advanced significantly since that time. Unfortunately, the systematic differences in achievement that existed during that same time, although improved, continue to exist today.

Throughout the course of the last several decades, many attempts have been made to equalize educational outcomes. Among the more recent approaches is the use of assessment data to leverage educational change and increase accountability. One reason that this approach is popular to many people in the general population is that it seems to be successful in a business context. Also, who is against accountability? It would be hard to find many people—either academics or laypersons—who argue against accountability as a concept. However, as the saying reminds us, the devil is in the details.

While the success of a test-based accountability approach continues to be debated, much of that debate has focused on assessment and instructional considerations, policy debates, and the impact on academic outcomes. Only a small part of that debate has focused on how the day-to-day dynamics of the classroom are affected and what students and teachers experience and internalize on a personal level. Even less attention has been paid to these issues for students who are in the process of learning English, a growing segment of the school population. One of the key indicators of academic success in the current context of accountability is the ability to speak English.

This focus, when combined with the emphasis on assessment and accountability, has special consequences for English learners.

My interest in this book stems from my own conversations with teachers and my observations of English learner students struggling to deal with these new accountability demands. In my own work, for example, I have observed how accountability pressures cause some English learners to mask their inability to speak English. Many students experience school as a mix of accountability demands and strong pressure to speak only English. But these demands have also led teachers and schools to act in unintended ways, for example "teaching to the test," cutting out "nonessential" subjects such as creative writing and art, focusing teaching efforts on those students most likely to make gains on accountability measures, and so forth.

This book captures these and other aspects of current efforts to boost achievement and tells an important tale that cannot be conveyed by numbers and tables. It examines three important areas that are not often considered: English language learners (ELLs), mandated and highly structured curricula, and high-stakes testing. In doing so, it considers the student's and teacher's point of view and situates these practices within a larger policy context. While providing informative coverage of the technical issues related to high-stakes measures, the book also provides careful and detailed classroom observations. As an educational psychologist with an interest in motivation, it was difficult to read Ms. Romano's well-intentioned but unfortunate practice of posting each student's test scores, making each child's test performance the center of classroom discussion. Such practices are very reminiscent of the tracking and labeling practices of the "red bird" and "blue bird" reading groups several decades ago when I was in elementary school; the innocuous labels did not fool students then, and it is likely that current versions of these practices do not fool students now.

In summation, this is an important book to read. The author's argument is clear and well thought out; and while the reader may not agree with all of her points, it is thought-provoking and gives rise to many questions. It is important information for teachers; for those who depend on, employ, and train teachers; and for those who create the policies under which teachers are required to operate.

—Robert Rueda
University of Southern California

Preface

The argument of this book derives from my classroom observations of a fourth-grade teacher whom I will call Ms. Romano. All of the names I use in this book are pseudonyms, to protect the confidentiality of students, teachers, and administrators in the school district I describe. The project on which this book is based began as an ethnography of the school experiences of Ms. Romano and her students, told from their own perspectives. Ms. Romano was kind enough to let me sit in her classroom, talk to her students, ask her countless questions, and draw my own conclusions. When I told her I was going to write a book about my year in her classroom, she shook her head slowly and said, "It's not going to be good!" She knew, you see, that her teaching skills had been greatly constrained by her environment. I told her then, and I continue to tell her now, that I enjoy working with her because of her emotional connections with and respect for the children in her classroom.

Ms. Romano's students were eager to be heard and written about. They were happy to talk about themselves, their work, and their lives. The original impetus for this book was my desire to try and create better educational opportunities for students like them in the future. The book is organized around the larger themes of testing, classroom instruction, student lives, and teacher education. Each chapter offers a different perspective on what I see as a complex and thorny problem: how to disentangle ourselves from the accountability web in which we are trapped.

Many of the accountability pressures I discuss in this book are direct results of policies mandated by the No Child Left Behind Act of 2001 (NCLB). Partly in response to widespread criticism of NCLB's accountability system, the Obama administration called for NCLB to be revised in 2010. Policy makers failed to make headway on reauthorizing NCLB before the 2010 elections ushered in a Republican-controlled Congress. Ironically, in their desire for less federal oversight of schools, Republicans may want to make some of the revisions proposed by the Obama administration, such as removing the pass/fail system, strengthening charter school options, and increasing the role of student test scores in teacher evaluation and tenure. One example of this bipartisan desire for continuing, if not increasing, accountability is the case of Michelle Rhee, the former Chancellor of the Washington, D.C., Public School system. Rhee was hired by Mayor Adrian Fenty, a Democrat, and she engineered a rather groundbreaking contract with the D.C. Public Schools teachers' union that made teachers' evaluations and tenure much more reliant on student test scores. Rhee quit her job in October of 2010, but the union's contract stands. Recent developments in Los Angeles, which I discuss in Chapter 5, and across the nation, make the contract's tenure-breaking less newsworthy now than it was in 2010. In late 2010, Rhee accepted the offer of the Republican Governor-elect of Florida, Rick Scott, to serve on his transition team and help his administration sort out educational issues. It appears that her ideas are palatable to both Democrats *and* Republicans looking for solutions to accountability problems and pressures.

However, the Republicans want less federal oversight while spending less money. In my ideal world, this situation would lead to less testing, because testing is expensive. But this is unlikely, as testing seems to be an incontrovertible aspect of modern American schooling. Testing practices are deeply entrenched in our education system, and penny-pinching Republicans eager to rewrite the Elementary and Secondary Education Act (ESEA) will probably not make many large-scale changes. Indeed, the worst-case scenario is that things will continue as they are. As I suggest in this book, if we continue to rely primarily on standardized tests to show that our students are making progress, then those tests need to be overhauled in a variety of ways—and that is an expensive process unlikely to occur in a time of economic recession. These unpleasant possibilities are unfortunately supported by the arguments about accountability that I make in this book.

Acknowledgments

The clarity of this book is a direct result of the good-natured readings of various drafts by various people: my husband, Mihir Pandya; my father, Christian Zacher; my friends Maren Aukerman and Huong Nguyen; and my editors Meg Lemke and Susan Liddicoat. I'm particularly glad to be able to thank my husband, Mihir. Without him, this book would be littered with extremely long, difficult-to-parse sentences that seem to go on and on. The few that he and Susan missed are my responsibility entirely. I'm also very grateful to the ears of my friends JuliAnna Ávila, who repeatedly assured me my sanity was not at stake, and Laura Ruth Johnson, who listened to me kvetch at least once a week.

More direct thanks goes to my research assistant Valerie Perry, who took part in discussions about key events in the classroom during data collection. Thanks also go to my colleagues in the College of Education at California State University, Long Beach, for providing an intellectually supportive environment—especially my Department Chairs Felipe Golez and Dan O'Connor. The College and University supported me by providing time for gathering data and writing during different periods from 2006–2008. Finally, the John Randolph and Dora Haynes Foundation in Los Angeles supported me with Faculty Fellowships in 2007 and 2008. In the end, I can say that writing this book has been a lot of fun (especially now that it's over), and I'm glad all of these people were there with me for the journey.

OVERTESTED

CHAPTER 1

When Testing and Language Learning Are Synonymous

A list of student learning goals in English and Spanish dominates one wall of the office at Laurel Elementary School in Southern California. It reads:

Students will *write* to proficiency
Students will *think* mathematically
Students will *read* at grade level
Students will develop effective *oral language skills*
Students will *compute* quickly and accurately

When I first came to Laurel Elementary (all names are pseudonyms) as a researcher, I thought these goals were relatively unobjectionable. What teacher would *not* want their students to write proficiently, to think mathematically, and to read at grade level? As a literacy researcher, I was particularly interested in learning how writing, reading, and oral language proficiencies were cultivated and assessed. The longer I spent learning about the testing regime (35 tests per year in total) and strict language arts curriculum at Laurel Elementary, the more I saw objectionable aspects of these seemingly neutral learning goals. Eventually, I came to see this poster as a warning that at Laurel Elementary, testing, English language learning, and acquiring literacy skills were inextricably, and often unfortunately, intertwined.

Watching teachers teach and students participate, I realized that this poster's formulations of how and what students should learn incorporated ideologies of testing from the very beginning. Take the concept of *writing to proficiency*. On the English-language arts and mathematics portions of the California Standards Test (CST), the top two of five score levels are "Proficient" and "Advanced Proficient." English language learners (ELLs) comprised over 90% of the student population at Laurel Elementary.

Despite the fact that assessment experts caution against relying too heavily on the results of tests that are normed on native speakers with second language learners (American Educational Research Association [AERA], American Psychological Association [APA], & National Council on Measurement in Education [NCME], 1999; García, McKoon, & August, 2006a), the ELL students at Laurel Elementary were required to take the English-language CST. These suspect scores contributed to the school's Academic Performance Index (API) and Annual Yearly Progress (AYP) accountings. For the non-native speakers at Laurel Elementary, becoming a proficient writer meant, in essence, scoring at one of the top two levels on the English-language arts portion of a standardized test normed on native speakers' scores.

The goal of native-like fluency was further complicated by an incomplete definition of academic proficiency, measured by a somewhat arbitrary test score cutoff determined by the state (see Bracey, 2008; Ho, 2008; Sunderman, Kim, & Orfield, 2005). In addition to confusion over how to assess English language learners' proficiency in English, there is no clear consensus about the best way to teach academic English to ELLs. For instance, administrators at this school believed that ELLs could be helped by the highly structured language arts curriculum Open Court Reading (SRA/McGraw-Hill, 2000), a prepackaged literacy curriculum purchased widely in California in various forms since the 1970s. However, some researchers have found that prepackaged literacy curricula like Open Court do not necessarily help ELLs acquire English (Arya, Laster, & Jin, 2005; Cummins, 2000, 2007; Moustafa & Land, 2002).

A final clue about the links between testing and learning buried in this innocuous list has to do with the goal that "students will read at grade level." Language arts instruction at Laurel Elementary was focused on getting students to read on grade level, which made the state's Reading Benchmark test scores a teacher's main measure of a student's reading ability. There were two tests per grade, one to signify meeting reading benchmarks for the "middle" of the grade and the other for signifying the meeting of the benchmarks at the end of the grade. The emphasis on making progress on benchmark tests toward grade level left no room for the concept that reading abilities might develop differently, at different times, for different children depending on the kinds of language and literacy skills they had brought with them to school.

Teachers in schools with structured curricula are required to implement their materials with exacting fidelity to a master schedule. The detailed weekly plans Laurel Elementary's teachers followed (based on a combination of the Open Court teacher's manual pacing guide and the

Reading First-funded literacy coach's site-specific variations) were meant to lead students to achieve, and test at, constantly higher levels. Similar trends—of teachers pressed to teach quickly, to the test—are visible at other schools across the nation, wherever curricular mandates hold sway (Kersten & Pardo, 2007; Valli & Chambliss, 2007; Valli, Croninger, Chambliss, Graeber, & Buesi, 2008). Students were also supposed to pass the appropriate reading benchmark tests at the appropriate times (i.e., the Middle of Fourth Grade test in the middle of their fourth-grade year). Their scores were publicly posted in the classroom and the school; if children's scores fell too far behind, they were at risk of being retained in certain grades. Students and teachers almost always assessed reading abilities by the students' reading benchmark scores, and talk about benchmarks and score levels pervaded classroom and school life.

As my brief analysis of the Laurel learning goals poster shows, tests were central to the teaching of writing, reading, and oral language skills at this school. While there are many laudable aspects of our American educational system—free K–12 schooling for all children, well-functioning suburban schools, ongoing efforts to serve immigrant and language-minority children, to name a few—our passion for accountability has led us to testing for testing's sake. We test automatically, broadly, and often, instead of strategically, purposefully, and with precision. My data offer ground-level perspectives on this problem, and my findings suggest that, in order to understand the experiences of teachers and children in many American schools, we need to examine the current trend toward increasing accountability for schools and teachers through an integrated lens of literacy, language, *and* assessment perspectives. My findings also show that we will need to approach the problems I describe from this integrated perspective if we are to improve children's learning opportunities by making necessary policy changes.

In this book I focus on the effects of high-volume, high-stakes testing on classroom life; on the kinds of participation afforded and elided by the mandated curriculum; and on the lived experiences of students and teachers in such highly regulated environments. These topics require that I also address debates about how to measure linguistic (and other) proficiencies, the validity of different language assessments, the overuse of assessments, and the risks and benefits of teaching language arts to English language learners via mandated, structured curricula. Some of the events and practices I report in this book may seem incredible—as in hard to believe—especially to those who have not recently spent time in a public elementary school. However, all of them took place in a real, and expanding, culture of extreme accountability.

INTRODUCING THE CALIFORNIA CONTEXT

While some states—New York, for instance—allow districts and schools to make their own curricular choices, California schools must follow the mandates of the California Department of Education (CDE, 2006; Skindrud & Gersten, 2006). The CDE (2006) uses both national standards for curricular programs (i.e., reading programs based on "scientific" evidence) and its own set of needs and demands as the basis for approving curriculum for its approximately 1,050 school districts.

In the 2002 adoption cycle, the CDE approved only *two* programs for use with kindergarten through sixth graders: *Houghton Mifflin Reading: A Legacy of Literacy* (Houghton Mifflin, 2003) and Open Court Reading (SRA/McGraw-Hill, 2000). For the 6-year, two-program-only adoption cycle (during which I conducted my classroom study), school districts could use another program, but they had to pay full price for it instead of paying the subsidized price for either of the two approved programs. (Charter schools were also able to choose and use other curricula.)

In its most recent curricular adoption in 2008, the State Board of Education approved nine different Reading/Language Arts curricula and nine related programs for its English language learners, but more choice does not necessarily mean better quality. Unfortunately, many of California's less well-funded school districts lacked funds to purchase new curricula because the math curriculum adoption in the previous year left them with few dollars to spend on new language arts curricula. One coping mechanism was to officially adopt one of the new sets while applying for waivers from the state to continue to use preexisting Open Court or Houghton Mifflin curricula.

"SoCal," the prize-winning urban district in which I did this research, serves approximately 90,000 students, 40% of whom were and are English language learners. Some of its schools were ethnically, linguistically, and socioeconomically integrated, while others such as Laurel Elementary were much more segregated (Zimmerman, 2010). After a thorough internal review of the two possible curricular choices in California at the time of this study, the district adopted Open Court in 2002. The district had been awarded a Reading First grant in 2001 and had received federal funds from the program to staff its own Reading First office, whose employees (usually former teachers) worked as traveling mentors to support individual schools' Reading First–funded literacy coaches. These schools were required to use Reading First funds to purchase tests tied directly to each Open Court unit of instruction. The district's Reading First office personnel had aligned the required Reading First assessments with Open Court's six units, and students took six extra reading comprehension tests a year to meet the program's accountability demands. These tests were meant to demonstrate student progress to district and state Reading First officers. Though the interim (Gamse, Bloom, Kemple, & Jacob, 2008) and final reports on the program reported "no statistically significant impact on student reading comprehension" (Gamse, Jacob, Horst, Boulay, & Unlu, 2008, p. xxviii), at the time of my study, the SoCal district was fervently pro–Reading First.[1] The SoCal district's attitude might have been the result of the federal dollars that the district was given as a Reading First site. District specialists modified Open Court lessons for their English language learners in concert with some of the Open Court authors, and they also monitored teachers' use of their innovations. They prided themselves on using pacing guides to keep teachers and students "on track" and on the use of common assessments like reading benchmarks.

To impose and reinforce a common set of beliefs about poor children, the district required that incoming teachers read and discuss Payne's *A Framework for Understanding Poverty* (2001). The district also mandated that teachers use a set of eight graphic organizers called Thinking Maps™ (2004); teachers were required to display master versions of the maps on their walls, and were expected to use them daily in their instruction. The district also purchased and made principals and teachers implement what they called a "common teaching approach" based on Madeline Hunter's *Essential Elements of Effective Instruction* (1983). These programs were systematically introduced, taught to teachers in professional development sessions, and mandated. At different times, through tests and site visits, the district assessed teachers and students on the implementation of these teaching philosophies, approaches, and curricula.

For various reasons—perhaps including intensive teacher training in Open Court Reading—Laurel Elementary had seen several years of continuously rising test scores. In their review of effective reading programs, Slavin and colleagues (2009) found Open Court had promising results, but noted that the effects may be due to the extra professional development that went with the program. Dr. Spring, the principal at the time, credited some of the children's success to her teachers' strict implementation of the Open Court Reading program. Certainly the repetitive nature of activities and the fact that students encountered the same structure and patterns year after year contributed to their ability to do well on Open Court-related tests. The school routinely hosted visitors eager to learn about their Open Court successes. Before I had decided on a research site, I was one such visitor, looking for a classroom in which to observe.

I decided to conduct research at Laurel Elementary when I met Ms. Romano, a fourth-grade teacher. An immigrant herself who had come to the

United States speaking only Spanish, she had a great degree of empathy for her students' situations. Her high level of respect for her students seemed almost to supersede the difficulties I had already begun to find with the Open Court curriculum. We spent some time getting to know each other at the end of one school year, and I officially began to collect data at the start of the following year.

In her fourth-grade classroom, Ms. Romano had 28 students: 21 English language learners, 4 students who had been reclassified as Fluent English Proficient (or FEP'd), and 3 native speakers of English. She and most of her students spoke both English and Spanish, though English was the language of instruction. In 1998, California voters passed Proposition 227, a referendum that made it illegal for schools to teach ELLs in a language other than English.[2] Instead of transitional bilingual programs in which students were taught some content in their first language while learning English at the same time, transitioning to English within 3 years or so (see Crawford, 2004, for details), ELLs are now allowed only 1 year of Structured English Immersion (Baker, 1999), after which they are placed in regular classrooms and assessed in English only. Students can attend bilingual programs, but parents must sign waivers for them to attend, and to do so, parents must first be aware that the programs even exist.

Ms. Romano had only taught post-Proposition 227, and so was not subject to some of the concerns and problems as teachers who experienced the proposition's effects firsthand (Palmer & Garcia, 2000). Neither she nor her students had been exposed to methods of educating ELLs other than the 1-year newcomer class Laurel Elementary hosted for approximately 20 students at a time.[3] The newcomer class functioned as the school's Structured English Immersion class, and the number of students in it was capped. When a newly arrived ELL was assigned to the class, the most advanced ELL was moved out, with no student staying longer than 1 school year. It has now been more than 10 years since 227 passed, and California's Latino children continue to suffer from underachievement.

Laurel Elementary School was located in an economically depressed part of the city; approximately 90% of its students, most of whom walked to school from nearby apartments, lived in poverty. At the time of my study, Laurel was one of a handful of schools whose populations were so impoverished that the district did not require families to fill out free and reduced-price lunch applications; instead, it simply gave free meals to all students. The neighborhood was subject to several police actions a week. The school was periodically locked down when reports of gunfire or gang activity led the police to think it might be too dangerous for children to play outside on the playground. High rents and low wages contributed to some transience in the school population, and the number of students in Ms. Romano's class fluctuated as students entered and left.

In the year I spent in her classroom, Ms. Romano followed the pacing guide for Open Court with great fidelity. With the help of one of the Reading First-funded literacy coaches, she even engaged her students in some of the Open Court inquiry lessons, student-led projects that are supposed to be the culmination of Open Court units, but which are seldom taught. For instance, while Ms. Romano enjoyed the inquiry lessons and thought her students did as well, the pressures to complete each Open Court unit in certain pre-set periods of time meant she was seldom able to "do" inquiry (Zacher Pandya, forthcoming, 2012a). She did attempt to set short- and long-term learning goals for and with her students, despite her uncertainty about what skills her students—English language learners and native speakers alike—were learning through the Open Court program. In Chapter 3, I present a detailed picture of language and literacy practices in her Open Court classroom. For now, I want to preview some of the ways testing, curriculum, and language learning intersected in everyday school talk.

IN MS. ROMANO'S CLASSROOM: SETTING GOALS FOR AND WITH ENGLISH LANGUAGE LEARNERS

In my year of observation, I learned that the school's admirable—if sometimes seemingly unattainable—goals were routinely echoed in classroom conversations. The following illustrative conversation took place between Ms. Romano and her students at the start of the school year. In it, she and her 28 students, 21 of whom were ELLs, began to set their own learning goals. It was only in retrospect that I saw how similar their learning goals were to the testing goals posted in the school office.

> Standing at the front of the class, Ms. Romano introduced the goal-setting exercise by reading aloud the first agenda item of the day: "Scholarly trait—setting goals." To introduce the idea of goals, she drew a quick sketch of a football field with an arrow pointing to the goalposts at one end of the field. She told students this particular icon meant *goals*, and had students cut out the small version of the goalpost illustration from papers they each had on their desk. While students, who were seated at clusters of four or six desks, cut out their own goal icons, Ms. Romano told me (but not her students) that she had learned about this icon and others like it from the teacher of the

gifted students. She said she wanted to use them this year with her students, none of whom were labeled gifted, to communicate her high expectations of students.

I had asked to study Ms. Romano's students' experiences with the Open Court Reading program because of her seemingly endless belief in the ability of her students to progress. She never indicated to them that they were not gifted in her eyes, even though none of them had scored above proficient on their end-of-third-grade California Standards Test and, in fact, their combined scores made them the lowest-achieving class she had ever had. The positive atmosphere she tried to create ameliorated some of the testing burdens the children shouldered, but only some of them. At the start of the year, I had little idea of how large those burdens would be.

As children pasted their miniature goal icons into new spiral-bound notebooks, Ms. Romano asked for volunteers to share their goals. Nicole, a native speaking, English-only Latina student with long brown hair and a wide smile, said her goal was "passing benchmark levels." Alejandro, another native English speaker, chimed in to tell the class that he was already "on the Middle of Fourth Grade" benchmark test, and that he wanted to go even further.

Ms. Romano told the class that she had a story for them about a student of hers who was now in middle school. She asked, "How many of you know what it's like to not speak English?" At least nine children raised their hands. Ms. Romano nodded several times, saying she also knew what it was like to sit a desk and not understand anything, because that's how it had been for her when she "first came here."

This sudden segue into English language learning might have seemed an abrupt transition away from Nicole and Alejandro's benchmarking goals, but, as events unfolded, it made perfect sense. Ms. Romano's parents had come to the United States from South America when she was 9, and like many English language learners, she spent almost a year in a *silent period* (Krashen, 1985), speaking to no one at school. Once she had begun to speak English, she taught her mother to speak it too. I later saw that she was using her own story (which the children had heard before) to remind her ELL students of their shared histories and to set the stage for her anecdote.

Ms. Romano said she would tell Enrique Ortega's story—she said she could tell them his real name because he had gone on to middle school. She said he had come to her classroom a few years ago speaking no English. She told him, "I speak Spanish," and said she asked him in Spanish what he wanted to do in school. He told her "*Yo quiero aprender*" ("I want to learn"). He started taking books–on–tape home with him; she would tell him, "Stop, you're done!" every so often, but he kept taking books home. She told the class that Enrique passed the kindergarten and first-, second-, and third-grade benchmark tests (two per year, per grade) in 1 year. With mounting excitement, she told her class, "I said [to Enrique], 'If you pass one more before the fourth-grade test itself, I'm sending you to the gifted class.'" She smiled, and then told the class that Enrique had graduated last year—from the fifth-grade gifted class.

In essence, Enrique wanted to learn, so he passed benchmark tests. He might have spoken no English when he arrived, but a mere 2 years later he graduated from the gifted fifth-grade class. Ms. Romano's retelling of Enrique's story fused learning ("*yo quiero aprender*"), learning English, and passing tests into an inspirational tale. She left the goal of passing benchmarks alone for now—though Nicole and other students did make that one of their goals—and turned to more immediate possibilities.

For homework, Ms. Romano explained that students would have to write and illustrate three different goals and "what you'll look like when you achieve them." She said, "Last night we drew pictures of ourselves as scholars. Here we're just brainstorming. What's a goal for today?" After a few minutes of listening to volunteered ideas, most of them larger than the initial daily goal she had in mind, she suggested they "set a goal today with behavior." She said she'd give students three goals to choose from, writing them on the board as she spoke: 1. to "be such a good listener" that your eyes are always on Ms. Romano; 2. to be "on task"; and 3. to "finish all your work." She repeated these choices a few times, asking students to read them for her and with her, and then she had students vote for their goal with their hands up high. Students began writing down their goal next to their pasted-in goalpost icon, and Ms. Romano walked around the room reading over their shoulders. As she walked and read, she reinforced their choices, saying things like "Natalia, I'll know all day long you'll be looking right at me—great!"

This minilesson reveals three fundamental facets of classroom life at Laurel Elementary. First, it hints at the deep, reciprocal relationship between learning and testing at Laurel. Ms. Romano's recounting of Enrique's story taught students that passing tests was a valid, reasonable outcome of a student's goal "to learn." She would occasionally return to Enrique and his aims in the first months of school, and students learned quickly enough to take up his goals as their own. Throughout the year, Ms. Romano's students frequently told me their learning goals, and they were always stated in the form of the number of benchmarks a child planned to pass by the end of the fourth grade.

The second aspect of classroom life foreshadowed here is the inculcation of the sort of scholarly traits that these goals implied the students were lacking: to listen and always keep one's eyes on the teacher, be on task, and finish one's work. The goals uncannily echo the typical participation structure of Open Court Reading lessons: whole-group, teacher-led activities in which the student's main job was to listen, choose from pre-selected answers, and follow directions. Payne (2001) argues that poor students lack such abilities. As I pointed out earlier, Payne's book was given to new teachers in the district as part of early professional development, although reviewers have shown it to be laden with stereotypes and misinformation (Bomer, Dworin, May, & Semingson, 2008; Gorski, 2006), such as conflating linguistic characteristics of some students of color with the language of students in poverty (Dworin & Bomer, 2008). Ms. Romano had read the book, and though she recognized some of its limitations, she found some useful ideas in it—particularly with regard to ways of instilling scholarly traits.

Third, this vignette suggests some of the tension Ms. Romano felt between the demands of her principal and district, on the one hand (e.g., to implement Open Court Reading faithfully, to test frequently, to teach skills like being a good listener), and her own conscience, on the other (e.g., maintaining high expectations, celebrating students' successes, and conscientiously preparing them for the *many* tests she knew they would have to take). As I observed her teaching and became acquainted with her professional goals, I watched her wrestle, often to no clear conclusion, with her teaching context's competing demands.

In this book, I make the case that, like Ms. Romano, we as a nation have come to no clear conclusions about the best ways to teach and assess English language learners. I believe this is because we have not yet taken a comprehensive and cohesive enough perspective on the entirety of their classroom experiences. We have a growing research base on methods of assessing language proficiency (Abedi, 2008; August & Shanahan, 2006b). We know that holding deficit perspectives on poor children will not help them to acquire language and literacy skills.[4] We have ample proof that mandated, structured curricula do not serve most children well.[5] What we lack, however, and what I attempt to provide in these pages, is a sense of how these often segregated issues interlace, what their conjunction means for research, and how such knowledge can be applied to classrooms.

ORGANIZATION OF THE BOOK

While much has been written about the separate issues of English language learners, high-stakes testing, and structured curricula, we do not know very much about how ELLs and their teachers experience the multiple stresses of tightly-paced, deprofessionalizing curricula amidst the constant pressures of high-stakes tests. I have structured each of the main chapters of this book around the experiences of adults and children living at the confluence of these areas, contextualizing my own research in the SoCal district within a national, and sometimes international, conversation.

Appropriately enough for a book about accountability, I start by taking a look at testing in Chapter 2. I discuss accountability and surveillance practices in the context of testing ELLs. I describe the ways that accountability pressures foster disjunctures between what research strongly suggests teachers ought to do and what policies require them to do. These pressures lead to test-oriented teaching. In addition, they have created a context in which teachers have access to both too much and too little data about ELLs. In this chapter, I illustrate these effects by analyzing four major language arts tests to emphasize connections between language arts instruction and testing of ELLs.

In Chapter 3, I look at the research base propelling the rise of structured curricula and the ideologies for and against them. Next, I draw attention to the particular ways prepackaged curricula limit learning opportunities for ELLs, especially when they are used in high-stakes testing environments. My analyses of representative literacy events—a read-aloud, independent reading, and opportunities to write—demonstrate the consequences of the use of these curricula with ELLs.

The many differences obscured by the label *English language learner* are explored in Chapter 4. I use case studies of students to make some claims about the differential consequences of high-stakes testing and structured curricula on students' classroom learning and sense of self. I elucidate these problems and offer some solutions.

In the beginning of Chapter 5, I discuss the disparities between teacher preparation and the actual teaching practices in which new teachers must engage in the field. Educated to implement balanced literacy programs and support ELLs via differentiated instruction, new teachers often discover that they are required to teach with one-size-fits-most prepackaged curricula.

Furthermore, their perceived effectiveness is increasingly based on students'
test score gains. At the end of the chapter, I discuss the growing research
base on how to best educate and support teachers of English language learners. What we know about teaching ELLs is often lost in the larger accountability pandemic, and I argue that policy changes at the federal level are the
only real solution to several dilemmas raised in this book.

In the sixth and concluding chapter, I look at changes to policies and
practices that would help ameliorate the current situation I describe. Requiring only one standardized, large-scale content-area test per educational level
would free up both time and money. Further, I discuss key policy changes
that are needed in the assessment of English language learners in the areas
of identification, data gathering and progress monitoring, test reliability and
validity, and accommodations. I also recommend ways to work with teacher
education programs to make key—and necessary—changes. Finally, I return
to the implications of accountability pressures for research, teaching, and
learning.

CHAPTER 2

High-Volume, High-Stakes
Testing in Elementary Schools

The burdens of assessment that students and teachers face in the United States are only partly the result of the accountability mandates of the No Child Left Behind (NCLB) Act of 2001. It would be more accurate to say that these burdens are symptomatic of a national obsession with accountability. Teachers and administrators find themselves caught in this cultural shift, unable to escape the educational mandates that politicians and policy makers have devised, and required to assess the progress of native speakers and English language learners alike. Increasing numbers of U.S. students come from homes where English is not the first language (García & Cuéllar, 2006), and their academic accomplishments are mixed (Kao & Tienda, 2005; Valdés, 2001). The need to accurately discern what these students know and can do in English intersects with the nation's anxieties about the growing diversity of our population and the globalization of our faltering economy. The assessment of ELLs in this somewhat tense context is complicated by two issues: Our knowledge base about how best to assess ELLs is only partial,[1] and assessment processes are financially burdensome and time-consuming for school districts.[2]

My goal in this chapter is to look closely at assessment practices in schools with high volumes of high-stakes tests. I suggest that accountability pressures create disjunctures between what research suggests teachers ought to do and what federal, state, and district policies require them to do. The resulting policy-driven assessment mandates have three effects. First, they lead to test-oriented teaching. Second, they normalize testing practices in schools to the degree that tests—and their results—seem incontrovertible. Third, they create a situation in which teachers have access to both too much test score data and yet too little information about their students.

ACCOUNTABILITY AND SURVEILLANCE IN THE ELEMENTARY CLASSROOM

One legacy of NCLB sure to continue in any revision of the Elementary and Secondary Education Act (ESEA) is our current web of complex statewide accountability systems (Vinovskis, 2009). Starting in 2006, all states began to provide report cards for their schools (National Center for Education Statistics [NCES], 2009a), and at least 45 states have longitudinal data-collection systems in place (NCES, 2009b) as part of their accountability efforts. In the largest-scale public school accountability effort the country has ever seen, the U.S. Department of Education requires states to publicize the number of schools not making adequate yearly progress (NCES, 2009c). It is essential to note that NCLB let each state set its own passing levels; therefore, it is at this moment impossible to accurately compare AYP percentages, which vary widely.

For instance, the District of Columbia (122 schools) and Idaho (626 schools) are the worst offenders, with 75% and 73%, respectively, of their schools failing to make AYP. California's percentage of 33 is average, though it has many more schools than most states (9,683). Other states with large numbers of schools show a range of percentages of schools failing to meet AYP: Texas (7,111, 9% failing), New York (4,470, 20%), Illinois (3,792, 24%), and Florida (3,226, 66%). One of the mandates of the Race to the Top Fund, the Obama Administration's first attempt to redesign education policy, was that states all assess their schools according to the same nation-wide standards/score bar.

I contend that our accountability systems and their potential punishments for failing to show progress—whether each state has its own standards or all aim for the same national bar—have created an environment in which research-based practices are often sidelined or ignored for the sake of showing growth (Ravitch, 2010). Let's take the state of California as an example (or a cautionary tale). California's system, the Academic Performance Index, is based on annual results from a variety of standardized tests: the California Standards Test, the California Alternate Performance Assessment (CAPA), the California Modified Assessment (CMA), and the California High School Exit Exam (CAHSEE) (Education Data Partnership, 2009). The state of California sets its own passing levels and applies them to the API as it chooses. Numbers for API scores and AYP are visible through school-, district-, county-, and state-level reports on the website of the CDE (2007). Under Title III of NCLB, students' scores on the California English Language Development Test (CELDT) are also reported as one of the state's Annual Measurable Achievement Objectives (AMAOs).

The public pressure on schools to make progress was tangible at the level of the classroom. One public accountability measure I frequently observed at Laurel Elementary was the sharing of test scores; sometimes the teacher would tell the class everyone's scores, sometimes they would be posted on a classroom wall, and sometimes they would be listed in the school hallways. This practice, encouraged and sometimes mandated by the principal, acclimatized children and teachers to talking openly about test scores by the time they left the first grade. Class discussions about individual students' test failures and successes were common, and helped to make test score progress (or failure to progress) a regular and normal part of classroom conversation. After some (but not all) of the Reading First Skills Assessments, Ms. Romano had her students share their scores with the class and analyze the class's performance as a whole. Students could score Advanced Proficient (AP), Proficient (P), Partially Proficient (PP), or Not Proficient (NP) on these Skills Assessments. The fallible logic behind sharing test scores was that students would understand their test scores in context and, as a result, try harder to do better the next time. The first time I saw this happen, 12 of the 28 students in Ms. Romano's room had just scored 5 or below out of 10 possible points, or Not Proficient.

> Ms. Romano called on each student, wrote their initials on the board, and wrote their scores (which ranged from 1/10 to 9/10) on the board under their initials. Ms. Romano had already helped students think of encouraging things to say to their peers, which they did, along the lines of "good job, José," (6/10), "keep up the good work, Carlos" (8/10). Even Tara, who had only gotten 1 out of 10 possible points, was also congratulated—"way to go, Tara!"–as part of Ms. Romano's efforts to create a positive atmosphere even in the face of very low scores. After writing all of the numbers on the board, she then proceeded to mark the APs, Ps, PPs, and NPs in different colors. As Ms. Romano marked the three AP scores, she said, "Should we give them a big hand?" and the class did so. The Proficient group— four students—also got applause. She described the Partially Proficient (PP) group of nine students in this way: "Like you almost understood it, but not quite?" and several of the PP students nodded in reply. For the others—the 12 who scored only 5 or below—she simply said, "All the rest of the people . . . who just thought the story was . . . who just found the story to be really hard, [are] non-proficient."

This regular practice of score-sharing and analysis, in which students were made to see and compare their scores with their peers and also count the numbers of scores at each level, held the potential for moments of public humiliation. However, the Reading Benchmark progress chart Ms. Romano was required to post in her classroom was a permanent marker of shame. On this poster, students were listed alphabetically by first name, and their progress on reading benchmarks was marked with horizontal bars. In order to make her students feel a sense of progress—especially those like José who had started the year two grades behind, or at the End of First Grade—Ms. Romano had colored the benchmark tests passed before fourth grade in green, and colored the tests passed while students were in her class in red. José would go on to make 2 years of (testing) progress under Ms. Romano's tutelage, but despite these advances, at the end of the year he was still behind the district's expected score for a fourth grader (End of Fourth Grade).

In one of their many goal-setting conversations, Ms. Romano had asked students to set their own benchmarking goals, and Carlos, who started the year at the Middle of Third Grade, set himself the goal of being at least at the Middle of Fifth Grade level by the end of the year. He achieved his goal, and his progress was documented on the chart for all to see and remember, though he was always quick to point out the one other student who had surpassed even his goals. Ms. Romano told the class stories of past students who had set themselves such goals and accomplished them—including Enrique Ortega, the successful student mentioned in Chapter 1—and would go on to tell her future students about Carlos, who surpassed himself partly because of his strong desire to "benchmark ahead," in his own words.

These classroom surveillance practices were not the only ones enforced at Laurel Elementary. Throughout the school a visitor would see large (6' x 8') posters with titles such as "We Passed Mid-3!" (a reference to the Middle of Third Grade reading benchmark test). There was in fact one poster for every benchmark test from Middle of Kindergarten to End of Fifth Grade. Students' names were placed on the appropriate poster, and the name tags were color-coded by grade level so that all fourth graders' names were written on, say, orange cards, although those far below grade level were simply not included. Name tags were moved along as students passed the tests and as teachers or literacy coaches remembered to do so. Occasionally, one would see an out-of-place color in a group from children like Carlos, who benchmarked ahead and had their names moved to the next grade's poster, or from children like José, who were left behind.

The effects on students and teachers of such relentless, schoolwide surveillance and accountability were often easy to see, if hard to stomach. Students' self-esteem slowly eroded, as they resignedly accepted their low scores and the labels that came with them. For instance, Tara, the lowest scorer (1/10) on one of the early Reading First Skills Assessment tests, had to say "I got a one" in the whole-class score-reporting event described above. Her eyes were downcast and, though Ms. Romano (and later I) tried to make her feel better with platitudes, she could only repeat, in an ever-fainter voice, "I got a one."

Another easily visible (but hard to measure) effect of the public posting of scores was Ms. Romano's slow loss of composure over time and across testing events, to which I was witness. Between the principal's requirements to talk about students' scores in class and to post scores on classroom walls and school halls, and teacher meetings to analyze scores and discuss strategies for recent and future tests, teachers such as Ms. Romano described feeling overwhelmed, overtested, and out of touch with more teacher-centered methods of assessing her students (Llosa, 2007). Although this situation was surely unintended by the writers of NCLB, it is certain that the pressure to publicly account for progress—and failure—of students has helped to create such scenarios in schools across the country.

SORTING OUT THE EFFECTS OF STANDARDIZED TESTS

While it might be impossible to avoid all standardized testing in the United States, it is clear that we do overuse these tests and that they provide too much data that is not easily translated into pertinent and timely information for teachers. One of the sources of this overuse and misuse is a lack of federal oversight for the kinds of tests in use (Toch, 2006), despite the federal mandate to test. Standardized tests are summative assessments that offer a snapshot of what a student can do at a particular moment in time; they can assess certain kinds of comprehension skills, but certainly not all of the ways of thinking in which we might like students to be able to engage.

While summative tests generally cannot directly inform instruction, they are useful for tracking the progress of individuals and groups, provided the assessments are valid for the given population. However, the teachers with whom I work would agree that they should not be overused. In fact, teachers of English language learners often doubt the veracity of the standardized test scores of their ELL students (Pedulla, Abrams, Madaus, Russell, Ramos, & Miao, 2003).

Recent research on classroom assessment (Black, Harrison, Lee, Marshall, & William, 2004; Marzano, 2006; Popham, 2008) suggests that teachers and students ought to be engaged primarily in formative assessments of students' "ongoing work to monitor and improve progress" (Black & William, 1998, p. 148). The term *formative* describes assessments in which teachers and students engage together that are meant to *form*, or shape, subsequent instruction. These might include, but are not limited to, brief conferences, checklists, portfolios, and student self-evaluation (cf. Goodman, 2003). Formative assessments are intended to provide teachers results around which they might make curricular modifications in order to address knowledge or skill gaps that the assessment reveals.

Laurel Elementary is a case in point: Each of the main major language and language arts tests at the school was summative, and there was neither the time nor the administrative support for formative assessment practices. The tests I describe are high-stakes in the sense that, if students failed, or did not show enough progress, they might face retention. The stakes are even higher at the school level, at which point No Child Left Behind sanctions for failing to make Adequate Yearly Progress could place a school on the Program Improvement list, where they would be vulnerable to district or state takeover if they continued to fail to improve. In order to understand the implications of high volumes of high-stakes tests for learning and teaching,[3] it is necessary to look closely at what each high-stakes test measures, what is done with its results, and its effects on instruction. I use both the past and present tense in my discussion of these tests, because although some have been discontinued, many are still in use—though sometimes with different cutoff scores and consequences.

The California Standards Test

The high-stakes California Standards Test has two parts, English-Language Arts (ELA) and Mathematics, and students' combined results are the main measuring tool of California's accountability system. Gains and losses in a school's CST scores contribute to the school's AYP and its API, so overall score changes in either direction are of interest to administrators, teachers, parents, and policy makers. Many states' NCLB-mandated scoring systems allow them to claim greater progress on state standardized tests than their students have made on the National Assessment of Educational Progress (NAEP), but the Obama administration has changed the score reporting and valuing system so that all states now have to meet the same minimum federal standards (http://www2.ed.gov).

Like other standardized tests in use across the nation, the use of the CST to test English language learners in California shows its limited utility as a summative tool: This annual test is entirely in English, and all students, even newcomers to this country, must participate (although those here for fewer than 3 years may have certain accommodations made for them [U.S. Department of Education, 2003]). The National Literacy Panel (August & Shanahan, 2006a, 2007) and the Standards for Educational and

Psychological Testing (AERA, APA, & NCME, 1999) caution that using tests normed on native English speakers with ELLs can lead to test bias because results may reflect ELLs' English proficiency rather than their content knowledge. However, NCLB's Title I requirements force U.S. schools to test *all* of their students on tests like the CST (a requirement I address in Chapter 6). This kind of disjuncture between research and policy, in which research is ignored or overlooked, happens repeatedly in the realm of testing ELLs. It is one of many consequences of a national turn toward accountability and assessment, and the larger social anxieties these trends represent.

The ELA section of the CST measures reading comprehension, spelling, grammar, and vocabulary skills, as well as (in the fourth grade) students' competence in writing narratives, summaries, information reports, and responses to literature. Both the CST and its companion California Writing Standards test, given in the fourth grade, affect the instruction students received by fostering test-oriented teaching of writing. Students began practicing for the CST (given in April) starting as early as October, completing timed essays to increase their writing stamina, fluency, and speed. Given the many constraints the Open Court Reading program's pacing schedule placed on any kind of writing in the language arts period, the little writing instruction students received was almost exclusively geared toward the four kinds of essays they would write for the exam: narratives, summaries, information reports, and responses to literature (CDE, 2008). Overall, the aim of the writing they did produce was to generally engender increased speed and, more specifically, practice the test's essay formats.

Since CST scores are not reported until the end of the school year, they are mainly used in schools to foster conversations in which teachers and the principal talk about what they could and should have done differently and what they would do differently the following year to increase student scores. In such a fashion, next year's students would supposedly receive the benefits of Ms. Romano's analysis of this year's scores. Theoretically, because Ms. Romano knew her incoming students' scores, she could focus interventions on various subgroups, trying, for example, to move Far Below Basic scorers up at least one level. But, in practice, the scores were months out of date when she received them and were meant to be analyzed as summative measures of progress, not as tools for revealing students' intellectual capacities.

The California English Language Development Test

In post-NCLB United States, the goal for English language learners is to reach *proficiency* in English. In California, this proficiency is assumed when a child previously classified as Limited English Proficient (LEP), based on answers on their Home Language Survey (HLS) form, passes through all five score levels of the California English Language Development Test and is reclassified as a Fluent English Proficient speaker. Although home language surveys and English proficiency tests have different names, many states rely on similar proficiency equations (Abedi, 2007; Bailey & Kelly, 2010; Dúran, 2008). The proficiency mandate thrives even though the concept of proficiency itself is highly problematic, and measuring it is even more so (Abedi, 2008; Abedi & Gándara, 2006; García, McKoon, & August, 2006a, 2006b; Solórzano, 2008). Linguists argue that because language is an open system with many possible ways to state a similar idea, a standardized test like the CELDT that asks for one right answer is incapable of completely assessing a speaker's true competence (cf. Lantolf & Frawley, 1988). Indeed, while the CELDT purports to measure oral and literate English skills and to indicate when a child is proficient in them, the field of second language acquisition/bilingual education has yet to come to agreement on what, exactly, proficiency *is* in a second language (Cummins, 1981; Lantolf & Frawley, 1988; Lesaux, Geva, Koda, Siegel, & Shanahan, 2008). And, even if we *could* come to agreement, as Abedi (2008) writes, "there is no specific indication of which tests or which cutoff score would indicate an acceptable level of English Proficiency" (p. 21).

Despite a lack of consensus over the meaning of language proficiency and how to measure it, NCLB's Title I and III mandates have made schools responsible for finding a starting point and for measuring progress in some way; hence the deployment of the CELDT and other English Language Development (ELD) tests like it. These tests—in Arkansas, Iowa, West Virginia, and others, it's the English Language Development Assessment; in Oklahoma, Vermont, Wisconsin, and Washington, D.C., it's ACCESS for ELLs—generally link to core content standards, emphasize academic language, and cover four domains: listening, speaking, reading, and writing (Abedi, 2008). Most ELD tests have at least three scoring levels: beginner, intermediate, and advanced. Test results are used by federal and state departments of education to monitor the progress, and eventual reclassification, of ELLs from Beginning English speakers to Fluent English Proficient status.

Language proficiency tests such as the California English Language Development Test create accountability pressure on two fronts. For students, the CELDT is high-stakes because until a child or youth is reclassified as a fluent English speaker, or FEP'd, through the test, his or her access to upper-level classes is limited, particularly in middle and high school. It is also high-stakes for states and school districts, because NCLB mandates that they be judged according to how many of their students progress through

English language development levels and how quickly they do so (Abedi, 2008; Solórzano, 2008). The pressure to make progress is exacerbated by incomplete or unclear policies about how long students should take to become fluent English speakers. Hakuta, Butler, and Witt (2000), for instance, show that students take 5 to 7 years to become fluent in the kind of academic English needed to function fully in school. States often do not specify how long students should be labeled as ELLs; instead their focus is on the progress of ELLs from one level to the next, to show progress on NCLB's Annual Measurable Achievement Objectives.

The accommodations states can make for testing ELLs, legislated during U.S. Education Secretary Rod Paige's tenure, are supposedly reasonable, but no one has defined the term *reasonable,* or even the term *accommodations,* for states (Wright, 2006). At the moment, states may make up their own definitions and policies of inclusion and exclusion, leaving out lower-scoring subgroups when it suits their needs (see also Duncan, 2009). In addition, Kieffer, Lesaux, Rivera, and Francis (2009) have recently found that accommodations are "largely ineffective in improving the performance of the majority of ELLs on large-scale assessments" (p. 1190). Amidst this confusion, teachers like Ms. Romano seldom know whether or not their students' scores will even be counted toward NCLB compliance (Zellmer, Frontier, & Pheifer, 2006).

Like California Standards Test scores, California English Language Development Test scoring did not occur in real time. Students' scores were therefore of little immediate use to classroom teachers (Walqui, Koelsch, Hamburger, Gaarder, Insaurralde, Schmida, Weiss, & Estrada, 2010). Students enter a classroom with their prior year's scores attached to their names, and despite any progress they might have made in the intervening months, they keep the label until the end of the following year. For example, Ms. Romano was required to use students' CELDT scores to form leveled instructional groupings all year long, despite the fact that students' scores were at least 3 months out of date when she got them, and students might well become more proficient during the course of the year, requiring potentially less instruction in English language development. In one classroom of 28 students, 25 of whom were English language learners, she might have equal numbers of students spread across the score levels from Beginning to Advanced, as well as some who had already been FEP'd (moved to fluent English Proficient status) and some who were classified as native speakers, but, because of bilingual home lives, exhibited speech and writing patterns characteristic of second language learners. To support teachers like Ms. Romano as they attempted to differentiate instruction for their students, the district had recently begun a new language arts program meant to help differentiate instruction for each ELD level. It required teachers to ask ELLs specific reading comprehension questions based on their CELDT score level, and gave exact lengths of responses they should expect. The purpose of such differentiation was to help teachers ask students comprehensible questions and for teachers to know what might constitute acceptable answers from ELLs at different levels. However, in what will become a common refrain in this book, there was seldom time to implement such level-specific questioning in addition to the amount of directive teaching Ms. Romano had to do just to follow the school's highly structured and tightly paced Open Court Reading instructional plan.

Reading First Skills Assessments Unit Tests

As a Reading First school with a high percentage of students living in poverty, Laurel Elementary received extra federal funds. The school used the money to support two literacy coaches who helped teachers implement the Open Court Reading curriculum. In order to show that the Reading First money was being put to good use, teachers had to administer and track student progress on five Skills Assessments a year. Teachers were required to administer these accountability measures after each Open Court unit, which meant they did so approximately every 6 to 8 weeks. The tests were divisible into chunks for ease of administration. They assessed skills in fluency, reading comprehension, reading "skills," spelling, vocabulary, writing conventions, genre, and writing "traits." Each test was high-stakes, because each was a measure of both how well Ms. Romano had taught the skills that were supposed to have been conveyed in each Open Court unit, and how well students had understood and were able to display them. Ms. Romano administered the tests to the class herself, giving students approximately2 hours per subtest to make sure they had plenty of time to "do their best," an often-repeated phrase in her classroom.

The district's own Reading First office tracked Skills Assessment scores by school and teacher, and there was always a potential threat of censure if students did poorly, although no teacher at the school knew precisely what form the censure would take. One of the main problems Ms. Romano faced was not a fear of reprisals, since they were only nebulously identified, but rather a problem with accessibility. The texts used in the tests were often difficult for her ELL students to decode, let alone *comprehend*. Alvarez and Corn (2007) report similarly frustrating outcomes with their ELL students, who performed poorly on the very same Skills Assessments in a northern California school; like Ms. Romano, they as teachers "only knew that [students] were struggling," but "not with what or how to support them" (p. 359).

Theoretically, students' scores indicated to Ms. Romano how much they had learned from each Open Court unit. In reality, most of her students' scores fluctuated up and down throughout the year, without any clear pattern of rising scores but perhaps—if one looked with an optimistic eye—an overall rising trend. Practically speaking, Ms. Romano's students lost hours of instructional time during each test she had to give, and she was pressed to complete each Open Court instructional unit in a set number of weeks in order to be able to administer the test on time and report results to the district's Reading First office. Ms. Romano hurried through each unit, administered the Reading First tests, and could review her students' scores—but the class had to constantly move on to the next Open Court unit. As with the California Standards Test and the California English Language Development Test, low scores indicated to Ms. Romano that she should tailor her teaching of the current unit so that students might do better in vocabulary or spelling the next time. It was an inexact sort of effort, and one for which she had little time, since she also had to finish the current unit and asses her students afterwards with another set of tests.

Reading Benchmarks

The last of the four major tests I discuss, the reading benchmarks, are linked to the state's language arts standards (Shin, 2004). The way in which they were used and the public reporting of students' scores added more strain to teachers who were already feeling pressure to help their students make progress. Students in California are supposed to take and pass two reading benchmark tests a year and can be retained if they are too far behind. Benchmarking practices are so ubiquitous in the SoCal district and across California that they have spawned a new verb, *to benchmark*, as in, "I'm benchmarking this week." These practices were different from the routinized CST, CELDT, and even Reading First Skills Assessment testing methods, but the pressure to progress that they fostered was equally intense.

The more casual administration method for the benchmarks added to the incorrect perception that the consequences of failure were not as severe as those of the CST or CELDT. A teacher or a literacy coach would administer the test one at a time, pulling children out of the classroom. If the teacher wanted a student's scores to rise, he or she might suggest that the child take more time to finish in order to answer more answers correctly. I also heard about proctors who might send a child back to the books with a suggestion to look at some of their answers because, if they didn't, the student "might not" pass. In this way, with some flexibility for teachers giving the tests, a student like José, who came in at the Middle of First Grade, was able to pass two benchmarks and make some progress. He ended fourth grade at the Middle of Third Grade, a feat Ms. Romano deemed was as important for his self-esteem as it was to meet the district's requirements. In the year after this study was completed, the principal and teachers compared student progress on benchmarks versus their progress on the new CST scores. When they found large gaps between the two, with the CST scores lower than benchmarks, benchmarking practices were changed so that teachers would not administer their students' benchmarks. They are now given by a presumably less-biased outsider—that is, someone less tempted to help students pass a benchmark by giving them extra chances to answer questions.

As with the other major tests students at Laurel Elementary had to take, the reading benchmarks were standardized and summative, providing snapshots of skills (as opposed to formative, offering information that would form and inform the teacher's immediate instruction). As a result, they gave Ms. Romano no precise information about students' strengths and weaknesses that would have been useful in her daily instructional planning. When a student in the middle of fourth grade passed the Middle of Fourth Grade benchmark test, it told others that Ms. Romano was doing something right—or, at least, that her students were making progress on their benchmarks. From the teacher's perspective, the main effect of the benchmark scores was related to their use as public accountability measures in the school, on the posters in classrooms and the hallways that I described in the beginning of this chapter.

A CLASSROOM CONVERSATION ABOUT TESTING

As my discussion of these tests shows, accountability pressures can all too easily lead to policy decisions contraindicated by research (e.g., using tests normed on English speakers with non-native speakers), test-oriented teaching, and, most injuriously, too much data that are of too little practical use. For each student, Ms. Romano had access to a plethora of scores—one from the CST, one from the CELDT, five from the Skills Assessments, and multiple reading benchmarks. But she was never sure which of these tests provided the most accurate picture of what her students could do and what they needed help in doing next (cf. Goertz, Oláh, & Riggan, 2009). To make matters worse, she had no time to informally assess students' literacy needs, in order to find out what skills or concepts they lacked this week that she could focus on for the next week, because she was too busy giving or preparing for another test another test. This preparation often involved practicing writing essays, or practicing learning how to choose the best response for a multiple-choice test when the passage was incomprehensible.

I want to revisit Ms. Romano's classroom to show the effects of testing on a typical classroom conversation. In this scene, she and her students were sitting on the rug talking about the Reading First–required Skills Assessment. Most students had taken these tests in previous years, but this was their first time taking one in the fourth grade. Ms. Romano began:

> "Right now we're about to do one more thing to show how you've learned, a Skills Assessment." She held up a booklet with purple edging and black lettering and asked, "Have you seen one before?" Some children nodded and said yes. Ms. Romano said, "Four years ago the state said there are some schools in California that are not reading." Then she asked—clearly expecting her students to answer in the affirmative—if at their school, Laurel Elementary, there were "a lot of kids who are not reading at grade level?" She nodded yes to her own question, and some kids said "yeah" in quiet voices. Ms. Romano agreed, saying, "Yeah, we do," and a child said, "But we try," and Ms. Romano said again, "Yeah, we do." After a pause, Ms. Romano continued: "They gave us a bunch of money. So we take these tests every 6 weeks to see if we learned, because they're giving us money. So you've been getting one every 6 weeks. Today, you're using [your] brain full on." Carlos, a high scorer on reading benchmark tests, exclaimed, "That's how you pass the benchmarks!"

Carlos's comment about using one's brain to "pass the benchmarks" suggests the degree to which students at Laurel Elementary had internalized such test-taking strategies' success. He and his peers had been taking a Skills Assessment test every 6 weeks since their first-grade year at Laurel, as well as the biannual reading benchmark tests, the CST, and (for most of them) the CELDT. To them, being evaluated on reading skills in such a fashion was routine; to them, test scores showed learning, or its absence. As they often said, if you used your brain, you would pass the test.

> Ms. Romano nodded at Carlos's statement and then said, "There are four different tests in here, one matters to me and to Dr. Spring [the principal]. It's the one about comprehension, where we show we know about what we're reading."

The Skills Assessment tests had four main sections: reading comprehension, skills, spelling, and vocabulary. It also had three writing sections and one fluency section, but, because of districtwide pressure to improve reading scores, and because students' fluency was also assessed on reading benchmark tests, the writing and fluency portions of this test received less attention. Note that the school's definition of reading comprehension, "where we show we know about what we're reading," was reiterated and taken for granted here. It's a very narrow definition that leaves little room for other conceptions of comprehension (see Aukerman, 2007; Stevens & Bean, 2007). Ms. Romano went on:

> "You can get a 10, perfect, a 9, or 8." As she talked, Ms. Romano drew the numbers 1 through 10 on the white board to her right. "This is what we do after [you take the test]—I put it in the computer. Then Ms. Johnson [the literacy coach] in reading looks at it, then Dr. Spring, and then me. If you get an 8, 9, or 10, ka-ching! This kid can read, they're advanced proficient, because this material is fourth grade."

From this and many other similar conversations, it became clear that Ms. Romano and her students assumed that their performance on tests would be publicly scored and disseminated. The ease with which Ms. Romano combined higher numerical scores with greater proficiency suggests how deep the correlation between progress and progressively higher scores had become. One of the main reasons that such correlations occurred was the sheer number, kind, and complexity of the tests required. Ms. Romano and her students spent so much time talking about, preparing for, and taking tests that they had few opportunities to think about why they were being tested so frequently, much less why standardized tests were the main measures of their academic ability and progress.

The ubiquity of testing, the correlation of learning with test scores, the constant testing of children and teachers, and the public nature of success or failure are not unique to Laurel Elementary: All of these are national trends that are on the rise. They will continue as long as the federal government continues to enforce accountability measures based on students' success—and failure—on standardized tests.

CONSEQUENCES AND SOLUTIONS: WHAT IS WRONG AND HOW TO FIX IT

The effects of high-volume testing that I introduced at the beginning of this chapter bear repeating: Accountability pressure filters down from the federal government (via states, school districts, and school principals) to classroom teachers and students. These pressures often lead to the implementation of policies for instruction and assessment that go against the grain of recent research-based recommendations for what works for English language learners. There are three main consequences: test-oriented teaching, the normalization of testing as learning in the classroom, and the odd phenomenon of too many test scores but not enough information. I address them each in turn, and then discuss the ways formative assessments should be used to guide instruction and planning for English language learners.

Test-Oriented Teaching

The first and most glaring consequence of the high volume of mandatory assessments in classrooms like Ms. Romano's is that teaching is always oriented to the test, whatever the next test is. Instructional hours that might have been used for more and varied kinds of instruction are irretrievably lost due to testing pressures *and* practices. This creates an environment of *curriculum narrowing* (Baker, Barton, Darling-Hammond, Haertel, Ladd, Linn, Ravitch, Rothstein, Shavelson, & Shepard, 2010; Hoffman, Paris, Salas, Patterson, & Assaf, 2003), where non-test-related learning activities are marginalized. It also creates circumstances in which teachers—and administrators—feel so pressured to show progress that they may help children cheat, raise, or lower cutoff scores (as in the state of New York, see Medina, 2010; see also Bracey, 2008; Ho, 2008), or even falsify results, all to show more progress than has actually been made (Gabriel, 2010).

In addition to the time required to give and take actual tests themselves, student and teacher time is taken up with practicing for tests, discussing strategies for doing well on tests, dissecting individual and group performance on tests, giving/receiving pep talks about low test scores, reporting scores to other children and adults, and (for Ms. Romano) writing reports on test score performance.[4] Indeed, in Ms. Romano's room, as in so many others, the required pace of administration of the Reading First Skills Assessments and the Reading Benchmark tests was so tight that it left her with no sense of which skills her students had succeeded in acquiring and which ones they still needed to work on.

Testing-as-Learning Normalized in the Classroom

A second consequence of overtesting is that the troublesome practice of testing-as-learning is normalized in the classroom. In a school like Laurel Elementary, the high volume of tests, combined with the constant discussion of test scores and how to improve them, meant that teachers and students equated students' test score levels with their capacities and abilities. This normalization produced a system of testing-as-learning in which testing practices were incontrovertibly justified and test scores were inarguably accurate measures of ability. Scenes of public sharing of test scores and public displays of progress have a cruel edge, especially when we as adult readers place ourselves in the shoes of 9- and 10-year-old children like Ms. Romano's students. In her study of children's understandings of their teachers' perceptions of their ability, Weinstein (2002) found that, even in environments without such public displays, children made "sophisticated, thoughtful analyses" (p. 90) of their classroom achievement hierarchies. In essence, children are acutely aware of perceived differences in their academic abilities, and they infer their places in the hierarchy as they watch teachers interact with students in the classroom. Their awareness of their perceived level in their classroom does not mean that displaying scores publicly is acceptable; on the contrary, in educational psychology terminology, such constant reminders of academic failure may well lead to yet more "self-debilitating" ways of thinking about oneself and one's abilities to succeed (Bandura, 2002, p. 270; see also Paris, Lawton, Turner, & Roth, 1991).

A testing regime like the one in place at Laurel Elementary perpetuates this kind of environment, and after just a year in the system, children come to believe that test scores encapsulate their true abilities. If one believes that children rise to the heights we set for them, it is unconscionable to let children think they are only as good as their test scores. This is especially problematic for English language learners, whose test scores on standardized tests normed on native speakers are most likely going to be below the norm. These tests assess ELLs' linguistic abilities and content knowledge at the same time, and they may be behind in either linguistic or content knowledge compared to their grade-level peers.

Too Much Data, Too Little Information

The third and perhaps most devastating consequence of high-volume testing is that teachers like Ms. Romano are oversaturated with test score data that they cannot readily use to inform their daily instruction. In essence, they have too much data and too little information. Ms. Romano would never be able to learn enough about what—and when—her English language learners were learning from her reviews of her students' test scores. This is because her efforts would not be guided by an understanding of how much progress students ought to be making, given their relative ELL levels, but rather by a constant sense of pressure that students have to make and *show* some kind of progress.

Formative Assessment: Some Issues

There are many, many research-based suggestions of ways to ameliorate these problems; they include proper ways to use data to track and reclassify English language learners, and ways to alleviate testing pressures on teachers. I close this chapter with a discussion of one immediately useful tool: formative assessment(s). Although there is an extensive research base on the use of assessments to inform the instruction of ELLs (August & Shanahan, 2006a, 2007; Goldenberg, 2008; Goldenberg & Coleman, 2010), accountability pressures in high-volume testing contexts provoke such disjunctures between policy and research that recommendations from these studies do not often filter down to pedagogical practice in classrooms like Ms. Romano's. For instance, most researchers would agree that neither of the English language reading tests I described above—the standards-linked Reading Benchmarks and the Reading First Skills Assessments—are appropriate for use in making high-stakes decisions about English language learners' abilities: they are inherently biased because they are written in ELLs' second language (AERA, APA, & NCME, 1999; García, McKoon, & August, 2006a, 2006b).

Although the failure of the Reading First program to help students make significant gains (Gamse, Jacob, Horst, Boulay & Unlu, 2008) has obviated the need to protest this particular Skills Assessment—with no more Reading First funds, the tests are no longer administered—there is always room for more summative tests to creep into students' lives in the name of measuring progress. For instance, students at Laurel now take three *trimester assessments* each year to measure their progress toward content-area standards, in addition to the ongoing biannual reading benchmark tests. We need to constantly remember that instead of subjecting English language learners to multiple tests that give incomplete and inaccurate information about their abilities, and, worse yet, fail to offer their teachers meaningful information, we should be urging and training teachers to use a variety of informal, formative assessments (cf. Black et al., 2004; Echevarria & Graves, 2003; Frey & Hiebert, 2003).

The most immediate, useful, and often free assessments are those in which teachers should engage regularly: interviews, checklists, inventories, portfolios, samples of work, dialogue journals and learning logs, anecdotal records, conferences, and student self-evaluation (cf. Goodman, 2003; Samway, 2006). Though these methods may be more time-consuming than standardized tests, and may seem less objective, they yield more information on individual student learning and teachers' practices. Frey and Hiebert (2003) call such "teacher-based assessment" necessary, as it is where "the principles of sound assessment and the practices of effective instruction merge" (p. 609).

Testing is not going away, but it could, or perhaps should, be pushed out of the way so that teachers can do what they are supposed to be trained to do: teach. Of course, to be successful at assessing students' academic growth through observation and one-on-one interactions, teachers need to have their own working definition of the knowledge bases they are assessing. Take literacy assessment. Teachers need to have had adequate training in language arts methods and an awareness of developmentally appropriate literacy skills to create a yearlong plan that aligns with their state's language arts standards. They can draw on their knowledge—of what their students ought to be doing at their grade level, and of what they plan to teach throughout the year—as they make and employ formative assessments of students' needs and progress. In such a scenario, the annual standardized test would be what it is meant to be, a measure with which to gauge overall progress, instead of a pressurizing event whose resulting scores are used by the teacher as a set of labels for instructional grouping.

Unfortunately, teachers of English language learners in such high-volume testing environments seldom have the freedom to create and maintain their own annual language arts curricular plans, much less engage in formative instruction to guide their teaching. Instead, they are given prepackaged curricula and are required to follow its dictates regardless of whether the needs of their students match up with the curriculum they are made to teach. When we look only at the testing of ELLs, and ignore the structured language arts curricula teachers are often required to use, our view is incomplete. We must consider the realities of testing, of learning English, and of teaching language arts all at the same time in order to understand the full range of pressures on teachers, and the full set of complications that require attention. To do this, in Chapter 3 I take up the curriculum and its attendant pressures and problems.

CHAPTER 3

Using Mandated, Structured Curricula with English Language Learners

Why do policy makers, administrators, and even some teachers prefer pre-packaged curricula? Districts adopt prepackaged programs like Open Court Reading for the ways they carefully introduce new topics and stories via a comfortable repetitive cycle of teacher read-alouds, picture walks, focus questions, and "wonderings," all of which are research- or evidence-based practices. Students often seem engaged with texts: ELLs and native speakers turn pages, talk about the story with their peers and the teacher, and write notes about their reading. However, time pressures and the constraints imposed by various pedagogical practices mandated by the curriculum and/or the school district limit students' opportunities for English language development. Each of the main literacy practices in which students engage in the structured curriculum classroom is undergirded by certain ideas about the purpose of reading and writing, and each fosters the development of certain skills and the elision of others.

In this chapter I synthesize current debates about reading pedagogy and analyze my own data to explore the pitfalls of using structured curricula with English language learners. I argue that the consequences of the curricula as they were used at Laurel Elementary and other similar schools were dire; first I'm going to look at how we got to this point, and then examine the daily literacy practices in the classroom.

THE LURE OF SCIENCE AND SUCCESS

Publishers of structured language arts curricula use the double enticements of science and success to claim that their products lead to reproducible, concrete results. The lure of this eminently marketable fantasy has won over district administrators, principals, and even some researchers and teachers. Both terms—*science, success*—require a little unpacking.

Science

In the highly contentious world of reading research, the phrase *scientifically based research* (SBR) is a proxy for a particular ideology about the nature and purpose of reading instruction and assessment.[1] From the perspective of some policy makers and reading researchers, structured language arts curricula built around scientifically proven methods are the best available programs with which to teach children to read. Pennington (2004) has referred to this as the "proven methods" versus "unproven fads" debate (p. 141). Certainly, arguments to support the use of structured curricula center on the existence of a research base that proves their validity, reliability, and success (National Reading Panel [NRP], 2000).

When the National Reading Panel's synthesis of research on reading was published in 2000, language arts textbook publishers took to heart its recommendations that students needed to master five particular skills to become good readers: phonemic awareness and phonics (also paired as alphabetics), fluency, vocabulary, and text comprehension. The NRP's members included "leading scientists in educational research," indicating from the start an emphasis on the science of reading. The panel only reviewed experimental or quasi-experimental research (no descriptive or ethnographic studies of literacy development), and the five rather discrete skills sets they ultimately endorsed seemed tailor-made to be encoded into prepackaged curricula. By 2002, companies like SRA/McGraw-Hill (publishers of Open Court), Harcourt Brace, Houghton Mifflin, and Scott Foresman/Pearson, among others, were touting the ways their products aligned with the NRP's list of critical skills. Indeed, state boards of education drew up their curricular guidelines based on the NRP recommendations, and publishers—who wanted to sell products—designed accordingly (Allington, 2002; Altwerger, 2005).

Various forms of basal readers—textbooks to teach reading that include many anthologized children's stories in their most recent iterations—have been used in American classrooms for over 100 years (Dole & Osborn, 2003; Luke, 1988; Pearson, 2000; Shannon, 1989). From the SBR viewpoint, today's curricula are much improved because they incorporate proven methods for teaching the basic skills necessary for reading success. Studies about the successes of individual curricula began to circulate for Harcourt Reading (Conner, Greene, & Munroe, 2004); Houghton Mifflin Reading (Swartz & Johnston, 2003); Open Court Reading (Borman, Dowling, &

Schneck, 2007; McRae, 2002; Skindrud & Gersten, 2006); and Success for All (Borman, Slavin, Cheng, Chamberlain, Madden, & Chambers, 2007), to list a few. The results of these studies were often included in meta-analyses of the success of different programs in teaching reading skills (Cheung & Slavin, 2005; Slavin, Lake, Chambers, Cheung, & Davis, 2009).

The persuasive discourse of the science of reading is self-fulfilling and circular: If there are five elements or skills needed for reading, and the curriculum teaches the five elements and assesses students on them, then, so the logic goes, the pedagogical methods that work best to teach the skills must be the methods that provide the best test scores.[2] Those who question this logic and oppose a reading-as-science perspective often find themselves left out of the conversation because they lack the right kind of logic with which to enter the fray.[3]

Some curriculum authors take scientism to its extreme. Take the school-wide reading reform program Success for All (Slavin, Madden, Chambers, & Haxby, 2009). Its creators describe their "multidimensional intervention theory" model called QAIT, for Quality, Adaptation, Incentive, and Time, with certitude:

> A key assertion in the QAIT model is that the elements are multiplicatively related to instructional effectiveness (IE), or the ability of a program or teacher to add value to children's learning:

$$IE = f(Q \times A \times I \times T) \text{ (p. 6)}$$

Can one get more scientific than to use algebraic formulas to display the effectiveness of a reading intervention/school reform program? Whether the curriculum works or not, its authors seem to be selling reassurance in the form of science.

To believe in the worth of these programs, one has to believe that the test(s) in use adequately reflect students' abilities. One also has to hold a definition of reading comprehension as a skill or set of skills that is assessable on a standardized test (i.e., the Gates McGinitie). For those in the SBR camp, yet another selling point is their "data-driven" nature. Many require the regular assessment of students, sometimes once a month, sometimes more, depending on the curriculum and the intervention model. The assessments are of NRP-related skills (phonemic awareness, phonics, vocabulary, fluency), and teachers must use the data to "drive" instruction and group children by level (of skill in one or the other item, though not necessarily in terms of reading comprehension skills; see Arya, Laster, & Jin, 2005). No longer is instruction driven by individuals' instincts; instead, assessments provide real data to show what students need to know to succeed, which brings us to the ways success is measured, defined, and used as a selling point.

Success

The success of structured curricula in raising students' test scores bolsters the claims of curriculum makers. For instance, McRae (2002) writes that the results of his analysis of the implementation of the Open Court Program in roughly 300 California schools "provide clear and convincing evidence that students attending schools using Open Court materials acquire basic reading skills faster than students attending demographically similar schools not using Open Court materials" (p. 1). Similarly, curriculum developers focusing on differentiation (Walpole & McKenna, 2007) and Response to Intervention (RTI) (Haager, Klingner, & Vaughn, 2007; Johnson, Mellard, Fuchs, & McKnight, 2006), programs touted for their success with English language learners, claim that when their programs are properly implemented, all children can learn to read at or above their grade level.

For a new teacher faced with a potentially steep learning curve in terms of classroom organization, pedagogy, and management, a language arts curriculum with a daily—and sometimes hourly—plan for the entire school year can seem like a boon (cf. Lee, Ajayi, & Richards, 2007). Success for All claims to give teachers "effective instructional strategies to maximize active teaching and learning" (Slavin et al., 2009, p. 6). Open Court Reading (SRA/McGraw-Hill, 2002) provides explicit instructions to follow for in-class differentiation: *challenge* lessons for those ahead of schedule and *reteach* lessons for those behind. Teachers do not even need to determine who is in need of challenging and reteaching—assessments included with the program help them know how to categorize students. The terminology of success is attractive, and the promise that teachers will be given all they need from the program, perhaps in conjunction with intensive in-service professional development, is beguiling.

OPPOSITION TO STRUCTURED CURRICULA

One problem for those who oppose tightly paced, assessment-heavy implementations of structured, prepackaged curricula like the one I will soon describe in Ms. Romano's room is the lack of a strong, straightforward narrative against catchphrases like *science* and *success*. One potential alternative, *balanced* literacy instruction, has not proven to be quite enough of an alternative (Pearson, 2004), probably because *balanced* is a loaded and non-neutral phrase in the reading field (Gunderson, 2009; Pressley, 2006).

The main bone of contention for those who oppose the scientism of reading instruction is that the National Reading Panel's results were biased because the panel only reviewed studies they termed scientific; therefore they only included a percentage of available literacy research.[4] In the United Kingdom, a similar argument has developed over the execution and findings of the Rose Report, which some claim was biased and poorly researched (Wyse & Styles, 2007).

Other problems in this contentious field, each of which I review below, have to do with misuse of the NRP's top five list by curriculum developers; arguments about assessments and data; teachers' concerns; and, finally, issues with the use of structured curricula with English language learners.

Undue Emphasis on the Parts of Language

Many in the scientifically based research field used the NRP's results to bolster their claims that children should be systematically taught the parts of language in the early grades (phonics, phonemic awareness, and vocabulary, as well as reading comprehension), and only then be encouraged to do things like literature study and writing in the upper elementary grades, after they have mastered the building blocks. Although researchers in the SBR camp often mention that being taught the parts of language is necessary but not sufficient, undue emphasis is almost always placed on teaching the parts over the whole, teaching fluency before comprehension, and privileging one standardized textual interpretation over others.[5]

Questionable Accuracy of Test Scores

Opponents of strict SBR approaches to the teaching of reading argue that tests—even small-scale monthly assessments like those required by many intervention programs—are not always accurate measures of what students know and can do. Test scores do sometimes go up when structured curricula are used, but those effects may be related to a variety of as-yet-undocumented factors: intensive teacher training; intensive surveillance of teachers at sites by coaches to ensure compliance (see Perryman, 2006); an increase in the sheer number of hours spent reading in language arts class; teaching to the test; and using curricula and standardized tests published by the same company (e.g., Harcourt Brace, which makes the Harcourt Brace language arts curriculum and sells the Stanford Achievement Test [SAT-10]). Because of these conflating variables, it is naive to believe that test scores offer proof of the success of prepackaged curricula.

For the moment, the testing loop in many classrooms is cyclical and excludes alternate pedagogies, and even alternate definitions of what ought to count as literate behaviors. If one assesses reading skills via students' knowledge of phonics and phonemic awareness, fluency, spelling, and vocabulary, one gets a picture of what students can do with the *parts* of language, but not what students can do with the *whole* of language. Reading, people in this camp argue, is and ought to be much more than these discrete bits—but the SBR movement has left children stuck with only the parts.[6]

Negative Effects on Teacher Practices

Another criticism routinely leveled at prepackaged curricula is that they can act as deprofessionalizing agents, deskilling trained teachers over time so that those who are required to use such programs for long periods lose, or submerge, their own skills in the face of "the manual" (Jaeger, 2006; Shelton, 2005; Valli & Chambliss, 2007). Though the Open Court Program teacher's manual is euphemistically titled the Teacher's *Edition* instead of manual or guide, its teacher's editions are some of the most directive manuals on the market. Attempts to build teacher-proof curricula can offend both new and veteran teachers because they insinuate that teachers' training and experiences have not prepared them adequately for the task of teaching children to read. Citing a small and often overlooked caution in the NRP report that mandated programs may reduce teacher interest and motivation to teach, Shelton (2005) shows how teachers using Reading Mastery in Florida are emotionally drained, frustrated, and on the verge of being deskilled by the curriculum.

Indeed, much recent research focuses on the boredom and condescension many teachers feel during and after the intensive trainings, coaching, checkups, and assessments that accompany prepackaged curricula implementations in high-stakes testing environments.[7] One of many underresearched areas is the *fidelity* of teachers to any kind of program, be it basal readers, whole-language trade books, or Response to Intervention models, when no one is watching (Dole & Osborn, 2003; Kersten & Pardo, 2007; Pease-Alvarez & Samway, 2008). While SBR curriculum developers claim that their programs are systematic and explicit, it is up to individual teachers to implement the programs. Often the only "proof" available to those who analyze the "success" of these programs is limited to a rise in student test scores (which is, as I have noted, a problematic construct).

Difficulties When Used with English Language Learners

The last set of problems with the SBR approach has to do with the thorny, complicated issue of how to best teach English language learners.

The tests used to assess progress in skills and in comprehension are in English, the language of instruction, not in learners' first languages. The problem is not that the tests should be in students' first languages; indeed, some students are not literate in their first languages, and so this would be of no help (August & Shanahan, 2007). The problem is that the results of tests given in a second language should always be viewed with some suspicion.

Tests written in a student's second language, taken by a student learning that language, do not give complete portraits of what ELLs are capable of in terms of reading comprehension or discrete reading skills (AERA, APA, & NCME, 1999). English language learners' ability to comprehend questions, as well as their ability to choose correct responses, may be complicated by language acquisition problems; that is, a reading comprehension test may measure English skills more than reading abilities in English. Some curriculum developers might argue that it does not matter whether tests in English are valid measures of what students know—the target language is English, and students had better get used to testing in it. The issue is that students are quite often grouped according to their test results, and these placements often lead them to lower groups, where they receive more remedial instruction, and from which they are less likely to move up (Cazden & Mehan, 1989; Oakes, 1986; Weinstein, 2002).

A final complication that opponents of structured curricula wrestle with is how to assess ELLs' progress without erring in this direction and perpetuating homogenous groupings that leave ELLs in perpetually more remedial settings. None of these counterarguments are simple to make, as they require extensive explication. Policy makers are more interested in the language of science and success than discussions of nuance and complication. As long as structured curricula hold sway, literacy practices like the ones I am about to describe will be the norm in many classrooms—not just in Open Court Reading school districts, but wherever prepackaged, SBR-based programs are bought.

INSTRUCTIONAL PRACTICES AND LITERACY EVENTS IN THE STRUCTURED CURRICULUM CLASSROOM

I argue that prepackaged curricula limit language and literacy learning opportunities for English language learners, especially when they are used in high-stakes testing environments. At issue here is not simply that classroom life is structured by prepackaged curricula—that's a selling point for many administrators and newer teachers. The problem is with the results: In most cases, classroom life is structured so that there are limited opportunities for student engagement with ideas and texts (Dutro, 2010), and only scant, stunted, and partial opportunities for English language development.

Findings from my research indicate that there are three ways to describe the problematic aspects of the prepackaged literacy curriculum on offer at Laurel Elementary and at so many similar schools in the United States:

- They require a reductive approach to teaching language arts skills.
- They are teacher-centered.
- They allow limited time for English language development because of strict pacing requirements.

My findings indicate that each of these aspects of the curriculum has its own consequences:

- Students come to see reading as merely a matter of finding the right answer in the text/book.
- Students follow directions, and never lead or take initiative in their learning.
- English language learners' skills may develop more slowly than they should, because of a scarcity of occasions for meaningful engagement with the English language in and around texts.

These consequences are partly a result of the strict time pressures under which most teachers in structured curriculum classrooms (with ELL or native speakers) find themselves. The flow of conversation and pattern of events in a typical day is shaped by extreme pressures to be on time, not to fall behind, to keep pace with the unit. Ms. Romano was required to be on the same page of the teacher's edition as her colleagues each day. There was just barely time to teach each lesson in a unit before administering the unit's Skills Assessment post-test. In addition to getting through the six main stories in the anthology, teachers had to make sure to teach the grammar, spelling, and word knowledge lessons (i.e., phonics for older children) embedded in each unit because those skills were also assessed on the end-of-unit test. Visit any structured curriculum classroom today, and you will hear time employed to legitimize all sorts of pedagogical moves.

Ms. Romano had few choices if she wished to keep her job and try to prepare students for the tests she had to administer. Strict monitoring by the school's literacy coach, her grade-level colleagues, and the principal ensured that she made efforts to engage students in each activity in each unit in accordance with the teacher's edition. The slightly less regulated classroom environments described by Irvine and Larson (2001), in which teachers felt some tensions between having to follow a program and wanting to "pick and choose" (p. 54), have for the most part given way to classrooms like the one I describe here. This change has come about as NCLB's demands for progress have made themselves felt; the more progress is needed, the more tightly controlled teachers' practices are (Valli & Buese, 2007). These changes are an expression of our cultural turn toward increased account-ability, which is instantiated in many classrooms by a move from flexibility and teacher choice to rigidity and strict pacing.

In such classrooms, students spend up to 3 hours per day in whole-class activities in which the teacher provides some scope for independence, but ultimately requires students to complete the same tasks within the same amount of time. Teachers may modify instruction for their second language learners by reducing requirements for those with lower ELD levels (as mea-sured by the not-entirely-foolproof California English Language Develop-ment Test) or other special needs. At Laurel Elementary, the day usually began with a morning program—the calendar, the weather, daily atten-dance—followed by 30 minutes of grammar. Then, it was time for at least 80 minutes of one or more "reading" activities: being read aloud to from the basal reader's anthology by the teacher, independently creating graphic organizers to preview a new story in the anthology, or reading from the an-thology in pairs or alone (often while creating more graphic organizers). In addition, on weekly testing days, up to 2 hours would be set aside—either during regular language arts time or after—for test-taking.

To illustrate the ideas about reading and writing that are embedded in these practices, and show what kinds of reading, writing, and language skills are developed as children participate in these practices, I narrate sev-eral literacy events in this section. As I describe and analyze events, I also note what kinds of literacy practices and perspectives might be elided by these mandated practices. I start where Ms. Romano had to start each new Open Court unit, with a read-aloud to her students.

Starting a Unit with a Read Aloud

The read-aloud session at the start of a new Open Court unit is de-signed to activate students' prior knowledge about the topic of study. At the beginning of the fourth-grade year, Ms. Romano introduced her students to the unit called Risks and Consequences with a short excerpt from Rosa Parks's autobiography (Parks & Haskins, 1992). Reading this two-page story aloud took an hour and a half, during which students sat and listened, answered teacher questions, and followed teacher directions, all in accor-dance with suggested activities in the teacher's edition. The vast majority of the exchanges followed the typical classroom pattern in which the teacher initiates (I), the students respond (R), and the teacher makes an evaluative comment (E) about their response (I-R-E) (Cazden & Mehan, 1989). This interactional pattern is amplified by teachers' manuals that tell teachers what kinds of questions to ask, as well as what kinds of responses they should expect from students. Ms. Romano began by attempting to activate students' background knowledge (following the teacher's edition prompts):

> She said, "To start our unit, we're reading a little story about Rosa Parks." Children started to raise their hands and whisper about Rosa Parks, and Ms. Romano said "Tell your neighbor." I eavesdropped on Natasha, who said "Black people . . . she gave up her seat and then went to jail . . . the police came and took her to jail." Then Ms. Romano asked the class, "Who was Rosa Parks?"

This is a typical I-R-E prompt: Ms. Romano surely knew who Rosa Parks was, and was checking to see if any of her students knew.

> Teresa answered, "That lady that . . ." and trailed off. Ms. Romano said, "She was a lady, yes." At another table, hands went up, and Ms. Romano called on Nicole, who said "She was a lady that, she wanted freedom, on the bus, Black people had to sit at the back."
> Ms. Romano asked, "Was this yesterday or a long time ago?" and five or six students answered, "A long time ago." Daniel said "like Martin Luther King" a couple of times, but Ms. Romano didn't answer him; she said instead, "I wasn't alive, you weren't alive, but a lot of other people were. In the place where Rosa Parks lived there were very strict rules." She drew a bus diagram on the board—a rectangle with little squares for seats, one for the driver. She said, "These seats in the front were for White people even if no one was there. These (she pointed to the back seats) were for everyone else." Natasha repeated, "Black people." Ms. Romano colored in the second row seat to represent Rosa Parks' spot, and said, "She should have gone back, but she sat in it and it was okay until a White man came in, then she said 'I'm just tired of moving.'"

This brief history lesson about segregation was based on a suggestion in the teacher's edition to give students background information: "In 1955, there was a very distinct separation between the rights of people of color and White people" (SRA/McGraw-Hill, 2002, p. 19M). Ms. Romano's augmentation of the lesson with a diagram of the bus was probably intended to help her students visualize the exact scenario. The question she asked next, about Ms. Parks's "risky behavior," was also prompted by the teacher's edition.

> Ms. Romano then asked, "That's a risky behavior—why is it risky to stay at her seat, Brian?" He said, "'Cause she might go to jail." When Ms. Romano asked if she had indeed gone to jail, four (or more) students said yes, she had gone to jail. Ms. Romano said, "This is the story she wrote herself about that day, [titled] 'You're under arrest!'"
>
> As she read the narrative, Ms. Romano stopped periodically to ask a question. In the last few sentences of the excerpt, Rosa Parks explains that she had not thought her actions would lead to an NAACP test case; indeed, she wrote, "I did not think about that at all. In fact if I had let myself think too deeply about what might happen to me, I might have gotten off the bus. But I chose to remain" (SRA/McGraw-Hill, 2002, p. 19 O).

At this point, after the 15-minute read aloud, Ms. Romano had more work to do. She had to link the story to the unit's theme without knowing how well her students had been able to grasp the main concepts of the story itself. She began by labeling the risk Rosa Parks took—refusing to give up her seat for a White man—but, as students' responses show, it was not clear they had understood the risk Ms. Parks took.

> Ms. Romano said, "This is the risk, what was the consequence?" Andrea replied "She go to jail." Daniel said, "She got off the bus." Ms. Romano clarified: "The consequence is what happened to her. She went to jail. What else?" No one answered, and she said, "What happened? Is Rosa Parks an important figure in American history?" Natalia raised her hand but did not get called; Ms. Romano asked, "Did more Black people start sitting in White seats? How'd that happen?" Monique (the only African American girl in class) was called on and said, "They seen her do it, and they think she was tough to do it, and they did it." Ms. Romano nodded at Monique's comment, then said, "After Rosa Parks was arrested, she got lawyers. . . . She changed it so that White people couldn't sit in the same seats, and schools, too, so that all kids go together now." She continued, "She took a risk of being arrested, and she changed history."

In the teacher's edition, after they read the story, teachers were instructed to "Ask students these questions," including "What was one of the risks Rosa Parks took by not giving up her seat?" Some "possible answers" were also supplied, e.g., "She could be arrested," (SRA/McGraw-Hill, 2002, p. 19 P). The need to hew to the required questions, and listen for "possible" answers, meant that there was little room or time to address students' other comments, such as Monique's intimation of a larger social movement connected to Rosa Parks's actions. There was also a rush to make the point clear—hence Ms. Romano's somewhat accelerated attempt to connect Rosa Parks's actions to school desegregation.

> Ms. Romano said, "Brian, Brian, what did we talk about today in [this] reading?" Brian, the one African American boy in class, said, "Black people, White." Ms. Romano nodded at Phillip, and asked, "The bigger idea—what is the main thing we talked about in reading today?" Someone—not Brian—replied, "Risks." Ms. Romano added, "Consequences, consequences, say it with me," and most students repeated it twice. Ms. Romano asked, "What's the word?" and they all said it again. Then she asked, "As an example of consequences, what's the first story we looked at?" Carlos said "Rosa Parks." Ms. Romano asked, "Why [is the story about risks]?"

Class conversations were rife with missed opportunities to discuss potentially meaningful social issues like relations between "Black people, White," in Brian's words. One culprit is pacing, which forced Ms. Romano to get through the story and get on to the next one. Another is the curriculum's tightly directed use of each story; not only was just one interpretation of events allowed, but alternate and side discussions were simply not on the agenda.

> Tara, who had apparently listened very carefully to the story and Ms. Romano's directed questioning, said, "Because she took a risk on the bus to sit in a White person's spot." Ms. Romano nodded and asked students, "And how many weeks [are we doing this unit]?" Several answered "Six." She repeated the number, and asked, "How many stories?" and several students said "six" again. Ms. Romano said "Six weeks, six stories." She said the next story was "'Mrs. Frisby and the Crows' [O'Brien, 1971], starting tomorrow, and you're going to love it!"

Sometimes Ms. Romano would spread introductory read-alouds like these over 2 days, but 2 days was the maximum amount of time she could take; questions or comments students might still have wanted to make about Rosa Parks' story were left to fade away.

The paucity of time for engagement with ideas and concepts for English language learners was palpable in these read-aloud sessions. Had Ms.

Romano even wanted to make the concepts of risk and consequence, let alone desegregation, more accessible to her students through extended conversations or even acting out the events on the bus (she did draw a map of the bus on the board to show the seating arrangements), there simply was not time. Students quickly learned how to tell if their answers were correct or acceptable in these participatory sessions, and they also may have learned that the teacher held the one interpretation of the book, and it was their job to read like she read, to come up with the answers she wanted them to provide.

Previewing a Story with Thinking Maps™

Ms. Romano was instructed by the Open Court teacher's edition to preview each story to activate prior knowledge, provide background information, and help students set their purposes for reading a new story (SRA/ McGraw-Hill, 2002). Previewing usually began with the introduction of a question from the teacher's edition, such as "What would the world be like if no one ever took a risk?" Following the directions in the teacher's edition, the next step was to take a picture walk through the story itself. In this case, the story was "Mae Jemison, Space Scientist" (Sakurai, 1995), the fifth of six stories in the unit Risks and Consequences.

During the picture walk, children were to create a Thinking Map (2004) with which they would organize the information they gleaned about the story on their picture walk. The particular Thinking Map in use in this event, a circle map, was one of a series of eight that the school district had bought. There were maps for organizing a sequence of events (the "flow map," see Chapter 4), for linking two sets of ideas (the bridge map), and for analyzing similarities and differences between two related ideas (a double bubble map). Teachers had been trained extensively on how to use the maps, and were required to routinely employ them in conjunction with Open Court reading activities like this one.

> After 20 minutes spent answering the question "Why is it risky to go into space?" Ms. Romano took an hour to walk students through the story. As the walk progressed, she had them fill out areas of the circle map with discrete pieces of information: genre, title, main character, what they could tell from the illustrations, connections (text to self, or T-S, text to text, or T-T, and text to world, or T-W), answer to the focus question, and one wondering. Most students' maps resembled pizzas: circles with many dividing lines radiating from the center, with the title of the story written in a circle in the center of the larger circle (see Figures 3.1, 3.2).

At the end of the hour, Ms. Romano told the class to add the areas for connections and focus questions on their circle maps. She directed their attention to the questions she had written on the board (which were also printed at the start of each story in the student edition): "What would the world be like if no one ever took a risk? Can you fulfill your dreams without taking a risk?" She directed students to "Put one thought you have here, . . . I want you to put a little 1 and circle it, and your sentence should start with 'If no one ever took a risk the world would be like . . .'"

Figure 3.1. Andrew's "Mae Jemison, Space Scientist" Circle Map

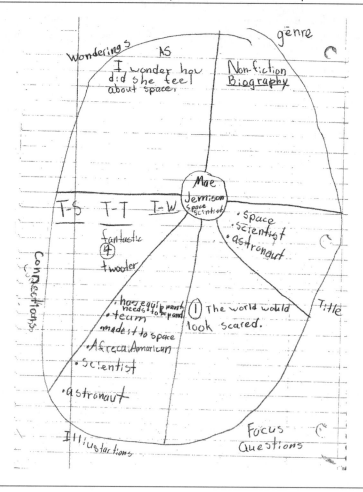

Figure 3.2. Teresa's "Mae Jemison, Space Scientist" Circle Map

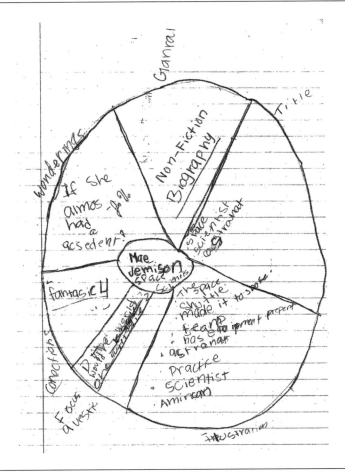

Many students began to share their answers. As they spoke, Ms. Romano told them they were "Just making a scholarly guess, hypothesizing" about what might happen if no one took risks. Some began with the phrase "The world will be" while others used "the world would." Some echoed worksheets by adding a long blank line onto which they would write in their answers (or to leave blank: see José's circle map, Figure 3.3).

I asked Carlos about his idea, and he explained: "It will be boring because maybe you wanna go hiking but you're afraid you might fall." After a moment, listening to the class conversation, he said,

Figure 3.3. José's "Mae Jemison, Space Scientist" Circle Map

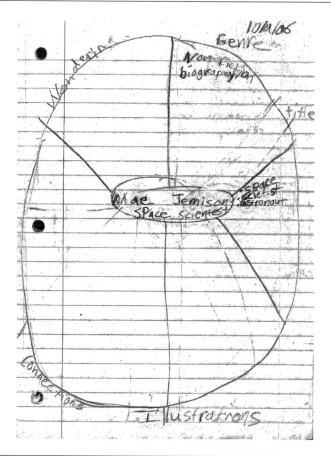

"Oh, yeah, I know," and erased what he had written so far about hiking, saying, "I have to put the word 'will be' first." He wrote "the word (sic) will be boring," but he did not write his idea about hiking again. He said aloud, "Because maybe you wanna go hiking but you wouldn't because you would be scared because of the big mountains." Ms. Romano, listening in, said, "Good, you understood!"

Andrew said, and wrote, "The world would look scared" (Figure 3.1). Teresa said "people will not die, you would not die," and wrote "The world would know (sic) one will die" (Figure 3.2). Andrew and Teresa both came into fourth grade labeled as Early Intermediate English Language Learners (level 2 of 5) on the California English

Figure 3.4. Crystal's "Mae Jemison, Space Scientist" Circle Map

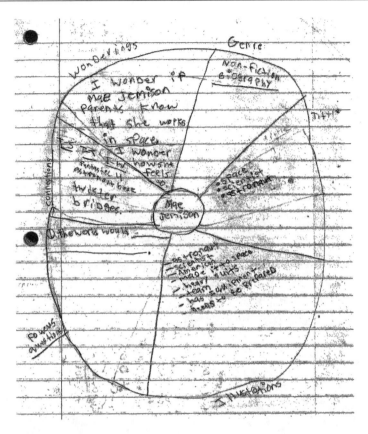

Language Development Test. For the most part, students like Andrew and Teresa could coast by in these activities, because they were usually just copying information from the board, the story, or their peers. José, a beginning ELL, looked around the table and said nothing. He had not made a space for Focus Questions but it didn't matter—he did not write anything down (Figure 3.3). Natasha, an Advanced (level 5) ELL according to her CELDT score, wrote in the prompt and a blank line, but also didn't fill it in (Figure 3.4). Nicole, an English Only Latina student sitting nearby, wrote, "the world would be dead because what if a fire got in your house and there were no fire man to save you!" (Figure 3.5).

Figure 3.5. Nicole's "Mae Jemison, Space Scientist" Circle Map

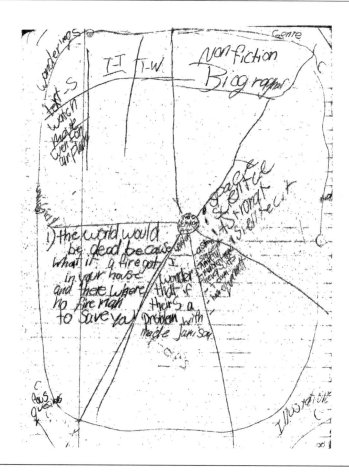

After a few more minutes of discussion and writing, Ms. Romano told the class they had to write "one wondering you have about the story—your ticket to recess." The teacher's edition regularly specified the use of a three-part reading transparency (transparency #41) on which to record students' thoughts in the preview period. The three columns on the transparency were Clues, Problems, and Wonderings. Ms. Romano had the latitude to instead ask students to put their wonderings on their circle maps. As she spoke, she wrote her own wondering on the board: "I wonder if Mae Jemison's parents were happy or worried."

Andrew wrote, "I wonder how did she feel about space" (Figure 3.1). Teresa wrote, "If she almost had a acsedent? (sic)" and then decorated her "wonderings" section with a friend's initials (JV in cursive, Figure 3.2). José labeled a space for wonderings but wrote nothing (Figure 3.3). Natasha had two: "I wonder if Mae Jemison parents know that she works in space" and "I wonder how she feels to" (sic) (Figure 3.4). Nicole, perhaps trying to instill some drama into the story, wrote, "I wonder that if theirs a problem with Made (sic) Jamison" (Figure 3.5).

The careful question and answer session, in which Ms. Romano had to continually push her students to the next section (from genre to what they learned from the title to what they learned from the illustrations, etc.), was structured by the time pressures she was always under. There was no time for Ms. Romano to follow up on individual comments, or to check to see if students' answers matched the "possible responses" given in the teacher's edition. Not that this would have necessarily been a good idea—publishing a rather predictable set of possible responses to given questions seems to give teachers even more incentive to make sure students are following the correct interpretation of the story. The resulting sameness of student replies—after the teacher made students erase, or take back, "impossible" responses—contributed to the narrow, teacher-centered nature of these curricula.

One of the problems with the way Thinking Maps like these circle maps were used in conjunction with Open Court Reading activities was that pacing pressures limited the kinds of feedback a teacher could give to students about their writing on the maps. A casual glance at a student's reading journal might suggest that they had done a lot of writing about stories—look at the text on Figures 3.1, 3.2, 3.4, and 3.5—but in reality teachers had no opportunities to help students augment or explore ideas, much less correct mechanical errors of spelling, punctuation, and grammar. There were also no consequences for not filling in the maps—José, whose map was incomplete (Figure 3.3), was able to go to recess along with everyone else. As a result, some students wrote just enough to get by (a lack of pressure to produce written products can be a benefit for beginning ELLs, but is not necessarily useful to more advanced learners). In addition, students like Andrew and Nicole, who seemed to have put a lot of thought into their replies, were no less or more rewarded for their participation.

The Thinking Maps create their own constraints on English language development. Take Carlos's decision-making process. I did not reproduce his circle map here because it was very difficult to read. He was so focused on what he "had to put" that he only wrote down about a third of the ideas he had articulated aloud about risk. In addition, he was more concerned with the structure and propriety of what he had to produce than with the content. He spent as much time erasing and rewriting his responses as he did thinking them up and writing them down. Like so many other tasks in this classroom, this one constrained his oral and written English language development.[8]

To make matters worse, although creating the maps required that students write copious amounts of text in relation to stories, the writing ended here. Students produced circle map versions of Thinking Maps for their previews of each and every Open Court story, and got to be very good at them, but they never wrote anything about stories based on the maps or the stories—they always had to move on to the next story and the next test. Students essentially drew handwritten worksheets, filling in the blanks after creating the blanks, so that even José, who wrote nothing, and Natasha, who left a blank for herself to fill in, produced written documents that offered the illusion of activity and engagement (Freire, 1970/2000).

Independently Reading a Story and Searching for Answers

Students did read stories in Ms. Romano's class; indeed, as the year went on, she got the children to be faster and faster at making pre-reading circle maps to make more time for reading stories and preparing for the unit test. On one occasion, I watched students spend 15 minutes making circle maps about a nonfiction text "Starting a Business" in the Open Court unit "Dollars and Sense." After reading the introduction, Ms. Romano turned the next section of the story over to the students. She asked students to find partners with whom they could work, and had them make lists that answered her—and the Open Court teacher's edition's—questions. I sat next to two boys, Juan, an English language learner with an Intermediate label, and Daniel, a former ELL who had been reclassified as Fluent English Proficient the previous year.

> The boys were making lists called tree maps, shaped like inverse trees, with one larger idea at the top, and then three subsections. They were working in the subsection on the left side of their pages, which Ms. Romano had told them to label "What do I like" and "What am I good at."

If this sounds confusing to you, the adult reader, imagine your chances of understanding the complexity of "what do I like" and "what am I good at" for an English language learner. Not only are these two separate ideas, but they are also phrased awkwardly. A sentence starter such as "I like to___" or "I am good at ___" might have helped. And having the boys put the phrases as separate categories might have also helped them sort ideas from the reading selection in the basal more easily.

> Juan read, and Daniel made three dots below the subtitle on the left (one for each paragraph in the subsection, I later learned). The boys proceeded to read the first paragraph aloud together, with Daniel correcting Juan as he read. Daniel moved ahead more quickly than Juan, which made for an uneven read aloud.
>
> Daniel said, "Let's write a list," and Juan asked, "How many the teacher said?" Daniel said, "Three, cause there's three paragraphs." Juan said, "I read this one, [it's] longer." Juan started reading again, and Ms. Romano said, "Freeze!" She told them to write about the first paragraph and then read on. She asked Brian and Phillip to share theirs—they had written, "Your business should be easy and fun." After this interruption, the boys continued to read, with Daniel reading the words "manufacturing" and "maintenance" for Juan. At the end of the second paragraph, Juan asked Daniel, "So what to—?" and Daniel said, "So what should we do? It's easier to start? You're already used to it? Yard cleaning, [it's] easier to start, cause we're just picking up things in the yard." Then he wrote "easier to start" and "used to it" on his paper, while Juan copied his list, writing "easier to start and usta (sic)."
>
> Daniel looked at Juan's page, and changed "usta" to "useta," then nodded, as if satisfied with his editorial efforts. As both boys read aloud, Daniel continued to correct Juan: requires, preparation, profitable, and artistic (though he read "artist" for this last one). Daniel said, "We should make things, like that's our business, we could make jewelry, or dog collars." Juan nodded, saying, "You sell them," and Daniel agreed: "You sell them, lanyards, you put them on your key chain, so that's what it says, we should make stuff." Daniel wrote, "We should make stuff" on his list under the joint subtitles "What do I like" and "What am I good at."

As an observer, I was somewhat flummoxed, because the boys' comments did not match up with their tree map's subtitle ("What do I like" and "What am I good at"). The boys, it turned out, were jotting down ideas about starting a business, which was the title of the story itself and of their Thinking Maps, instead of focusing on the subtitles they had just written down at Ms. Romano's behest. The three paragraphs in the text included injunctions to think about what you liked, what was fun, what you might enjoy making or selling, but either the boys did not connect the information from the text to what they liked and were "good at," or they misheard the prompt. The boys' cooperative behavior echoed the strengths evinced by children in Delgado-Gaitan's (1987) study of Mexican American children's home and school socialization: they were being imaginative, resourceful, and making collective decisions. However, these were not the kinds of skills the activity was designed to elicit. As Delgado-Gaitan argues, this kind of authority is dissonant with the kind of authority children work with at home, where there is space to negotiate tasks; but by the fourth grade, most had learned to just go along, as we can see below.

> At this point, as I was musing on the boys' misinterpretation and on the wisdom of their ideas, Ms. Romano came over to the pair. She listened and read over Daniel's shoulder as Daniel said to Juan, "So, like, what are we gonna, like . . ." when Juan cut him off, saying, "You should write a list of . . ." and Daniel ended, "of jobs." Ms. Romano disagreed: "That's not what it says, can you go back and read it to me?" Daniel and Juan read the subtitle together aloud, and then Daniel said, "So, like, we should make a list of what we like and what's better for our talent, things that you're good at, things that you like, things that?"
>
> Ms. Romano said, "Look here," and pointed to a spot on the page. After a minute they found the word "fun!" and all three said it aloud; Daniel saw "easy," and Juan read "easier for you to do," and Daniel said "like, good at!" Ms. Romano said, "Please put those four things down." The boys added the items to their lists, and shortly thereafter Ms. Romano raised her voice to signal the end of the period, saying students had "picked good partners."

On the surface this seems like a more individualized, and perhaps more flexible, literacy event. Juan and Daniel made a good heterogeneous pair, and we can assume that Juan made more progress filling out his tree map with Daniel as his partner than he would have made alone. However, the boys were essentially filling out another worksheet (incorrectly the first time), and were reading the segment of the story to get from the text what the teacher and the teacher's edition said they should understand. In many ways, they were learning that reading meant looking for the right answers to the teacher's questions in the text. Whether the answers made sense on their lists, or even to them, was not really their concern. The chance to make personal connections to the text by discussing "what I like to do," or to extend the book's ideas into their own lives by describing "what I am good at," was lost in the shuffle to fill out the map.

Opportunities to Write

In structured curriculum classrooms there are so many stories that must be read, and so many kinds of language lessons that must be taught and practiced, that writing gets short shrift (Dyson, 2006; McCarthey, 2009). In Ms. Romano's room, the following activities were students' main opportunities for engaging in extended writing:

- Cards and letters for special events outside of the prepackaged curriculum
- Responses to Open Court prompts about stories they had read
- Extensive entries in ungraded home writing journals
- Copying down information for their Open Court Inquiry units
- Writing timed *stamina* essays in preparation for the fourth-grade writing test (CDE, 2008)

Each of these practices had different potential audiences and pedagogical purposes, but they all evoked similar ideas about the purpose of writing. It was sometimes for communication, sometimes to show that one had learned the right answer, and sometimes to practice fluency in preparation for the writing test.

Cards for Mother's Day were drafted for specific recipients using shared prompts (e.g., "I love you because . . ."), then edited by Ms. Romano if time permitted, and finally transcribed onto pretty paper or glued onto a larger card. These were the most communicative literacy artifacts students produced. They wrote responses to Open Court prompts like "What risk did Toto take by leaving the herd to follow the moon?" just as they would have replied on worksheets, to show they knew the right answers. Ms. Romano could review responses and judge them against the "possible answers" provided; students' answers tended to contain similar content, displayed with different levels of English writing skill. To make up for the dearth of writing time in the classroom, Ms. Romano began assigning home writing journals midyear. Topics were assigned for homework: "How I want recess safety" or "My Cousin __." However, she did not have time to collect or read the journals daily, so potential teachable moments were often bypassed, and students may not have been clear about the purpose of the journals beyond increasing their writing fluency, a topic to which Ms. Romano repeatedly returned.

Students' written notes for their inquiry projects, which Ms. Romano started facilitating halfway through the year, were often fragmented bits copied directly from nonfiction library books or the internet, depending on the questions students were asking and the sources they used to find answers. Inquiry projects were a mixed bag; they were meant to be student-directed, but Ms. Romano had been coached to guide students to frame suitable inquiries. As a result, the projects, which related to the Open Court unit of study, were neither totally student-driven nor entirely teacher-centered (Zacher Pandya, forthcoming, 2012a). I have not reproduced the notes themselves here because there were not very many—the extreme testing schedule precluded doing inquiry projects with each unit. Notes were most often turned into student-made books, PowerPoint projects, or other group endeavors meant to showcase what students had learned; but, again, these projects were infrequently done because of time pressures.

The district-developed *stamina writing* exercises designed to prepare students for the fourth-grade writing test were as indicative of the range of students' writing abilities as any other assignment. Students were given a set amount of time—10 to 20 minutes—and told to write on a topic of their choice from a brainstormed list ("What I will do on my vacation," etc.). Students counted the total number of words at the end and divided the total by the time to get their Words per Minute (WPM) score. Entries often made sense if one read them aloud very quickly, but they were only used for counting words per minute, not for conveying a story or making sense. To give a sense of the texts students produced in a 20-minute timed period, I have made verbatim transcriptions, including capitalization, punctuation, and spelling errors, of the first few sentences of some samples.

Teresa (Early Intermediate ELL, level 2 of 5) wrote 309 words at 15.5 WPM:

When I am in vicatin I am going to go to Honduras to see my grampa and my sister. I will be going to the river they call it the soda river. It is called like that because the water looks like something to drink. I can not wate tile my vicatin for I can go there and have fun, and to go to a airplane it will be my first time being in a airplane.

Pablo (Advanced ELL, level 5 of 5) wrote 285 words at 14 WPM:

I am going to tell you what I am going to do in my faction I am going to the zoo because I only went their one time. Then when that day passed I am going to the city to buy stuff.

Nicole (English Only) wrote 520 words at 26 WPM:

What I'm going to do on my vichation is probley to pass a test and I think I'm going. And after that I'll read my books and beg my mom to the libary. So I think I still have my check out card and I used to go to that libary and after school I alwas go to that liabary then we had to move but I'm still close to it probley when my mom drives it probley will take like four minutes and last time when I went there they brought pets and everybody was in a little room and when I walked in there was a big, big snake and there was a seat in the front so I mite go to that liabary again...

Tara (English Only) wrote 406 words at 20 WPM:

On fecason I am going to see my ant She is comeing from Ogen [Oregon]. I Love to see my ant it is the best time of the year when she comes I Love to see my ant.

I have organized these from lower to higher California English Language Development Test score levels of students, putting Nicole, an EO whose parents spoke Spanish and English at home, next to Tara, a White girl with no language other than English. A quick survey reveals that students' words per minute scores have little relation to writing or English language skills. As with the other kinds of writing, Ms. Romano had little time to consult with individual children or conduct minilessons on specific kinds of errors after such writing activities because of the aforementioned time constraints. There was even less time for her to understand what specific skills her students lacked and what kinds of practice they actually needed to make progress in their writing in English. As a result, writing like Teresa's, Pablo's, Nicole's, and Tara's went largely uncorrected. Indeed, students like Teresa reported feeling that they were good writers because Ms. Romano would occasionally write "good author" in their journal's margins when she read and responded in her monthly readings.

Of course, the main purpose of this assignment was to increase their writing stamina, or fluency, but, as we know, fluency is not everything—it *might* be necessary, but it is certainly *not* sufficient (Allington, 2009; Applegate, Applegate, & Modla, 2009; Paris, 2005). Writing many words per minute may be an especially useless, not to mention tedious, exercise for English language learners, who may struggle to express themselves in print on timed tests and may need more time to create meaningful narratives. As usual, in this classroom, the demands of the testing regime seemed to create dead-end writing assignments, while excluding more meaningful or extended writing. The demands of the Open Court implementation plan deepened this exclusion. These consequences meant that there was little room to help English language learners develop writing skills.

CONSEQUENCES OF USING STRUCTURED CURRICULA

There are many consequences for student learning when teachers like Ms. Romano are denied professional autonomy and are made to follow prepackaged plans. Children in such classrooms learn to see reading and writing as tasks that get accomplished by following teacher directions, looking for answers to questions in the right places in books, and filling in forms in the proper way. They often conceive of classroom knowledge as reproducible information instead of, for example, as skills that might be transferable from one content area or domain to another. I mentioned that there were three problematic aspects of these curricula, and I return to each of them here, pointing out places where opportunities are afforded—or elided—by different practices.

A Reductive Approach to Teaching Language Arts

My findings about the reductive nature of this approach to teaching language arts echo those of several other researchers (see especially Moustafa & Land, 2002; Valli & Chambliss, 2007). In the process of helping students to understand a story by going on a picture walk, or creating a tree map of ideas, Ms. Romano actually focused her students' attention on getting the right answers to her questions. Because Ms. Romano had to use the given questions, and because she had to move on to the next story within a predetermined amount of time, students were never allowed to interpret stories on their own terms. The prepared questions are not the ones she might have asked if she had been given leeway to create her own focus questions or wondering prompts to build on individual students' interests. The resulting answers were usually brief, even when students understood the questions.

In actuality some students' literacy skills were not up to the task of understanding Ms. Romano's questions, much less the reading selections, because they were often a year or more behind their grade level in terms of English skills. Juan, who struggled to make a tree map with his partner Daniel, was only one of many English language learners who was ill-equipped to meet Open Court's demands. For these students in particular, the need to find the right answer severely limited the kinds of interpretations they would or could make about stories on their own. For those who had been in the Open Court system for their entire school careers, like Carlos or Nicole, they had been so thoroughly trained that it is not clear how well they could interpret a story without a Thinking Map or a teacher to guide them.

Teacher-Centered Classrooms

I have argued that another, related aspect of these curricula is their teacher-centeredness that reproduces, almost word for word, the context that Freire (1970/2000) so eloquently described as *banking education* over 40 years ago. In it,

    (a) The teacher teaches and the students are taught;
    (b) the teacher knows everything and the students know nothing;
    (c) the teacher thinks and the students are thought about;
    (d) the teacher talks and the students listen—meekly. (p. 73)

As a consequence, students follow directions, and never lead or take the initiative in their learning. The curriculum, and its proxy ventriloquator, the teacher, are the center of classroom life, and in the name of pacing and timing, the teacher shuts students off, ignores student talk, hurries students up, and glosses over obvious misunderstandings (see also Durkin, 1978-79, for an example of these consequences). The perpetuation of the Initiate-Respond-Evaluate interactional mode is perhaps most damaging for English language learners, who, while they may quickly learn their role in the I-R-E exchange and how to interpret the teacher's evaluations of their comments, need alternate, open-ended questions and spaces in which to practice oral and written English skills.

LIMITED TIME AND AVAILABLE MEANINGFUL OPPORTUNITIES FOR ELD

Finally, and most damaging of all for students like those in Ms. Romano's class, these curricula afford limited time for extended English language development. There is, as the scenes above show, a scarcity of occasions for meaningful engagement with the English language in and around texts. As a result, ELLs' skills may develop more slowly than they ought. English language learners need opportunities for meaningful oral English language development, and there is a very limited space for such talk in structured classrooms. Children are often too busy following directions—or trying to—and are not given time or space to comprehend even the basic structures of some of the stories they are reading. Pacing is, once again, an enemy: Because of time constraints, there is little space for meaningful conversation because teachers generally have only one week per story, and have to read the story a certain number of times in the week, a certain number of ways, and must continue ever onwards. The stunted and partial nature of student talk around texts, and the similarly hazy texts students produce about books they read, are signals that these situations do not work for English language learners or for native speakers.[9]

IMPLICATIONS: WHAT TO KEEP, WHAT TO REMOVE, WHAT TO SUBSTITUTE

I do not believe we need to do away with basal readers. They do contain positive and useful elements: standards-based guidelines about what skills to teach when, rich children's literature, rich thematic units, and many phonics/phonemic awareness/alphabetics activities. Depending on how they are implemented, their usage can foster teacher collaboration. The narrow, teacher-centered, strict, and limiting aspects of the curricula—and curricular pacing—are the elements we must remove. English language learners need expansive, student-centered curricula. They need ample time for English language development. Their teachers need flexibility that current lockstep plans do not afford. Their teachers also need continued and more training in ways to meet their literacy and language needs. And although some changes can be made at the classroom level, it will take policy changes on larger scales to see these changes through. I end this chapter by mentioning a few possible positive changes. In Chapter 6 I discuss policy and practice changes more substantially.

Teachers like Ms. Romano, who must continue to use prepackaged, structured curricula, can work with their principals, literacy coaches (Assaf, 2005; Dooley, 2006), and grade-level colleagues to make mild changes that would help ameliorate this problem. These changes might include:

- More time for teaching each unit to relieve time pressures
- Extending beyond the given story to related stories at more accessible text levels for those with lower English skills
- Creating more time for meaningful writing activities related to stories
- Encouraging teachers to deviate from the script by asking their own questions and following up on their students' questions
- Allowing teachers to select several stories from within the unit rather than requiring that they cover all of them

The most important change would be fewer tests at the end of units and more cumulative projects in which students may express what they have learned in nontesting situations in which interpretation and thought processes matter more than getting the right answer.

Fang, Fu, and Lamme (2004) report on a project in which researchers and teachers worked together in a long-term professional development project to "make pedagogical transitions" away from structured curricula, with positive effects. One of the participating teachers wrote that "moving away from the basal . . . was scary. At first, I felt a loss of control, and I wasn't sure that I liked it. But ultimately, reading and writing became a much more challenging and exciting time than in previous years" (p. 58).

It is difficult to suggest remedies for the teacher-centeredness of a technocratic curriculum created to foster classroom situations in which students go along, for their own good. Changing this situation really requires that teachers step back from their roles as what Aukerman (2006) terms the *primary knower* and relinquish control, of discussions about texts at least, to students. This is harder than it sounds, because teachers and students have all been socialized into the I-R-E model. Teachers are often uncomfortable with wrong answers (Aukerman, 2006; Nystrand, Gamoran, Kachur, & Prendergast, 1997), extracurricular squiggles (Dyson, 1997, 1999), or even personal information (Dutro, 2010). When they are required to use a curriculum that makes their voices central, and when the curriculum is paired with assessments of reading skills, many teachers feel that they have no choice but to help students learn how to find the right answer, however they can.

There are, however, some things that can be done to make prepackaged curricula more ELL-friendly. The changes often require deviating from the curriculum, which (as with my other suggestions) can only be accomplished with the help and permission of principals and literacy coaches at one's school site. Best practices for ELLs include time and space to talk and engage with English in contexts in which the *right* answer is not the focus. Reading and writing activities should be meaningful to students, should offer some sort of intrinsic benefit or reward (Vygotskty, 1978), and should not be tied to high-stakes assessments that even newcomer students understand have power over their scholastic futures. In many cases there should be *fewer* traditional reading and writing activities, especially those with texts students cannot access, or those with Thinking Maps in which students simply copy and fill in blanks. In such circumstances English language learners would benefit more by leaving the curriculum behind, except for some of the discrete skill-building work.

Most important, I recommend making substitutions to expand literacy instruction into digital literacies, the arts, and critical literacy. Much recent research shows us that English language learners can have rich language and literacy experiences when they are allowed and encouraged to experiment with digital technologies (Ávila, Underwood & Woodbridge, 2008; Black, 2008; Hull, Stornaiuolo, & Sahni, 2010; Lam, 2005; Ranker, 2006; Ware, 2008; Ware & Warschauer, 2005). We also know that literacy practices can be profitably combined with art (Albers & Harste, 2007; Gude, 2009; Millman, 2009), drama (Smith & McKnight, 2009), and creative autobiography (Campano, 2007; Herrera, 2010; Lam, 2000) to engage students in scholastic endeavors. As I have argued elsewhere (Ávila & Zacher Pandya, forthcoming, 2012), critical literacy pedagogies can help prepare all students, including English language learners, for participatory citizenship in our globalizing world (Hill & Vasudevan, 2007; Janks & Comber, 2005; Larson, 2009; Morrell, 2008; Rogers, Mosely, & Folkes, 2009). Unfortunately, at the present moment, these are the kinds of literacy practices denied to English language learners by overly structured, tightly paced, high-stakes assessment-centered language arts curricula.

CHAPTER 4

Grappling with the Complexities of a Classroom of English Language Learners

There are many differences obscured by the label *English language learner*.[1] Take Ms. Romano's class. She had 21 students labeled as English language learners, but really had a combination of the following types of students (and even these groupings are broad and varied):

- Recent immigrants whose parents speak no English
- Those who have lived in the United States for 3 or more years and have Beginning or Intermediate scores on the state's language assessment
- Those who have lived in the United States their whole lives and have Intermediate to Advanced scores on the state's language assessment
- Those—immigrants or native-born—who have been reclassified from English language learner status to Fluent English Proficient (in California)
- Those who have lived in the United States their whole lives and have no ELL labels but are not, according to their teacher's estimation and their standardized test scores, proficient in the academic English they need to do well in school (Hakuta, Butler, & Witt, 2000; Walqui et al., 2010). These non-ELL students, often called English Only (EO) students, may come from homes where English is spoken, or they may speak another language at home.

How does a teacher in such a classroom go about helping each of these different students move along a developmental pathway towards greater English literacy skills and greater English language fluency?

FROM BEGINNER TO ENGLISH ONLY,
AND EVERYTHING IN BETWEEN

In this chapter I focus on five students from Ms. Romano's class—Teresa, Carlos, José, Nicole, and Tara—whose individual stories, taken together, showcase a range of issues related to the complexities of teaching English language learners in modern classrooms.

Intermediate, Average: Teresa

Teresa, who discussed her plans to visit her grandfather in Honduras in the writing sample at the end of Chapter 3, was in many ways a typical, average fourth-grade English language learner. She could be wildly full of energy and seem to take up more space in the room than physically possible, while at other times she would sit at the back of the carpet and fade quietly into the group.[2] Teresa came into Ms. Romano's room labeled as an Early Intermediate ELL, based on her California English Language Development Test score at the end of third grade (level 2 of 5). At that point she had spent 4 years in school in English, from kindergarten to the third grade. Teresa's Basic score (level 3 of 5) on the CST, the state standardized test in English, was above average. She had been learning English for 4 years in school (Spanish was spoken at home), and had 3 more in which to be reclassified as Fluent English Proficient. Most learners do not progress at a steady pace of one ELD level per year, but they should make progress over time, depending, of course, on the many variables that may affect their performance. Unfortunately, NCLB does not specify exactly what is supposed to happen to someone like Teresa if should she languish as an ELL past 7 years (Parrish et al., 2006; Walqui et al., 2010; Working Group on ELL Policy, 2010).

In class, Teresa preferred writing to reading, calling herself an "okay" reader who "gets stuck on lots of words." She felt that her teacher would say the same, and thought that compared to other students she was "sort of" a good reader because sometimes her scores were "higher" and sometimes "lower" than others'. Her surmises about comparisons and her teacher's judgments were accurate, according to the classroom benchmark chart and Ms. Romano's personal opinion. Indeed, I found that student and teacher perceptions of ability usually matched.[3] Teresa came to the fourth grade with a Middle of Third Grade reading benchmark score, not too far behind where a native speaker ought to be, and certainly further ahead on the benchmark chart than one might have expected of a student labeled as an Early Intermediate ELL on the CELDT. She actively sought to raise herself to the Middle of Fourth Grade by the end of the year, asking Ms. Romano's help in passing a benchmark before Mother's Day, so that when her mother came for the schoolwide tribute-to-mothers program, her "mom could see" her progress. If she continued to progress in her acquisition of academic English skills, and continued to be able to access the curriculum and learn the academic content in the next few years, chances were good that Teresa would at least make it to high school, perhaps by then reclassified as a Fluent English Proficient speaker.

Teresa was typical of most students in the class because she lived in impoverished circumstances. Her parents worked selling clothes at the local swap meet, and the family, whose numbers swelled from 8 to 10 during the year with visiting family members, lived in a three-bedroom apartment. The apartment was near the school, in a neighborhood of apartments, small stores, and restaurants with Spanish signage; few trees; and frequent gang activity and police actions.[4]

Figure 4.1 shows Teresa's drawing of "her" room, which was done as part of a unit on the book *Me on the Map* (Sweeney, 1998). She slept in a bunk bed with her sister (bottom left corner), and her parents slept on the larger bed, with the dresser between them. In the same room were the bathroom door, closet, couch, writing desk, TV, and a cousin's bed. Camarota's (2005) analysis of Census Bureau data suggests that "immigrants and their minor children account for almost one in four persons living in poverty" in America (p. 1). To state matters even more starkly, the poverty rate for immigrants is "50% higher than that of natives" (Garcia & Cuéllar, 2006, p. 2242; see also Gándara & Contreras, 2009; Hernandez, Denton, & Macartney, 2007). Teresa's situation, with several family members living together, sharing space and making ends meet, was the norm for many of her peers.

Socioeconomic status has an effect on English language acquisition, as well as on students' learning potential in general (Duncan, Yeung, Brooks-Gunn, & Smith, 1998). For instance, Hakuta, Butler, and Witt (2000) found that the English proficiency attainment of students at schools with more than 70% of students receiving free or reduced-price lunches (Laurel Elementary had over 90%) lagged behind that of their English-learning peers in schools with lower percentages of children living in poverty on measures of oral proficiency, reading, writing, and redesignation rates. Berliner (2006) argues persuasively that students' scores on standardized achievement tests are more indicative of socioeconomic status of parents than of inherent academic ability. The regular challenge of learning English that Teresa and her peers faced was exacerbated by unclear definitions of progress and the burdens and trials of living in poverty.

Figure 4.1. Teresa's Drawing of "Her" Room

Making Progress—But Is It Enough? Carlos

Carlos was easily the most personable child in Ms. Romano's room. She once said that she could put him at any table, with any group, and his presence would bring those around him to a higher level, academically and socially. He enjoyed schoolwork, enjoyed being with and working with his peers, and had pleasant, easygoing relations with almost everyone in the class. Although I saw him dispute ideas, I never saw him raise his voice in anger or fight with a peer. Carlos wanted to be a doctor or a teacher. He was planning to go to the same middle and high schools as his sisters, and then perhaps attend the local state college. (Thanks to an intensive college-awareness program in the district, students at Laurel Elementary had toured the local state college and community colleges.) He read across genres—science texts, storybooks, comedies, joke books that he got from school and the public library—and enjoyed reading and writing, although the texts he produced in class were not qualitatively different from those of his peers with similar English literacy skills. He would cite his reading benchmark scores to prove that he was a "good" reader, in his own words.

Carlos benchmarked ahead of his peers throughout the year, from the "normal" score of End of Third Grade at the end of third grade to the score of Middle of Fifth Grade at the end of fourth grade. The benchmark tests are supposed to measure attainment of reading standards; according to them Carlos was capable of engaging in reading skills that students should be able to display by the fifth grade. However, his CELDT score showed someone who might or might not be able to keep up in regular English lessons and reading, according to his Intermediate level. One of the confusions this engendered for Ms. Romano was that she had a student reading *above* grade level whose English skills were only Intermediate according to his End of Third Grade CELDT score. He scored a Proficient (level 4 of 5) on the CST at the end of third and fourth grades, making no progress on that test, but doing well enough (and scoring higher than the vast majority of his peers). One lesson to draw from Carlos's statistics is the unreliability of multiple test scores, especially for English language learners, for whom test scores in English are already suspect.

Carlos was from Mexico. His father had moved to the United States first, and was followed by Carlos at age 4, who came with his uncle, in what Hondagneu-Sotelo (2006) calls "family stage migration" (p. 39). His mother and two older sisters came later, at scattered intervals. I later learned that his older sisters and parents may have been here without legal documentation. To protect students' rights, and refrain from asking intrusive questions, I *never* hinted at the immigration status of a student or their parents; I only knew where they were born if they told me voluntarily, as Carlos had done. Carlos told me that his father had told him that coming to America was the best thing he had ever done for his family. Carlos's family life—with two sisters (who had both gone to Laurel Elementary), his mother, and his father at home together—certainly seemed more ideal than the mixed and refracted situations of some of his peers. However, his own legal status and that of his parents and siblings was undisclosed; his mother worked as a housecleaner and babysitter, and his father was a gardener.[5] His household members faced the stressors of living in a "mixed-status legal limbo" (Suárez-Orozco & Suárez-Orozco, 2009), with undocumented family members having fewer and different legal rights than family members who were in the United States legally (Gonzales, 2008; Hernandez et al., 2007; Suárez-Orozco, 2005).

Although it is unfortunately still statistically unlikely that Carlos will make it out of high school and go to college (Fry, 2003; Gándara & Contreras, 2009; Walqui et al., 2010), *if* he does, he and his sisters would all be eligible to pay in-state tuition in California regardless of their citizenship status. California State Assembly Bill 540 of 2001 makes undocumented youth eligible to pay in-state tuition if they meet certain other requirements. But if

they had been (and thus still were) undocumented, they would not be able
to legally apply for jobs after they graduated (Gonzales, 2008). In the more
immediate present, the fear of deportation of undocumented family members
was always present. Should a family emergency call a parent, aunt, or sister
back to Mexico, their return to the United States might be impeded by a lack
of papers, and the family might become even more fractured.[6] Carlos was not
alone in this situation; other classmates also lived with, or potentially were,
undocumented immigrants. Certainly transnationalism was a regular feature
of life for most of his peers, who had family in at least two, if not more, countries (Camarota, 2005; Capps, Fix, Murray, Ost, Passel, & Hernandez, 2005).

Carlos spoke English at school and Spanish at home and was literate
in English, but not in Spanish. When asked, Carlos said he spoke mostly in
English to his friends at school, even those who spoke Spanish, because he
worried that his peers who did not speak Spanish would not know what he
was talking about. Following an unfortunately typical pattern of language
loss, the longer Carlos continued learning only English at school, the less
likely he would be to acquire Spanish literacy skills (Cummins, 2000; Fillmore, 2000; Gándara et al., 2010; Wiley & Wright, 2004). Indeed, he had
no option to acquire Spanish literacy skills. This was due partly to the effects of Proposition 227 in closing down many bilingual programs once offered in California, and partly to his parents' desire for him to learn English
and succeed in school.

Carlos's parents were as involved in his schooling as they could be, given
their busy work lives. His mother was a frequent attendee at school events, including a read-aloud-to-parents day, field trips, and the Mother's Day celebra-
tion for which he wrote a special card. Like the parents in Menard-Warwick's
(2007) study of Nicaraguan immigrant households, Carlos' parents drew on
a variety of resources, including their own Spanish literacy skills, to support
their children. Deficit perspectives on Latino parents paint them as less interested in mainstream conceptions of educational success and more concerned
about their children acquiring good behavior and morals, referred to as *edu-
cación* (Goldenberg & Gallimore, 1995; Ogbu, 1991; Valdés, 1996). Carlos's
case shows a different reality, one of engaged, interested parents who want the
best for their children, echoing the findings of Goldenberg, Gallimore, Reese,
and Garnier (2001), Olmedo (2003), Olneck (2009), and Reese (2002).

Far Below Basic: José

The case of José presents different problems. He was an immigrant like
Carlos, and an ELL like Carlos and Teresa, but his academic progress was
slower than either of theirs had been, and he was at risk of retention and

referral for special education services. José intrigued me from the start of the project because he was very focused in class but never produced as much text or talk as his peers. In my observations and interviews, José's personality remained somewhat elusive. He was by all accounts very shy. He and one sibling had immigrated from Mexico with his mother when he was 6, and they had lived in California and attended Laurel Elementary for the past 3 years. Like many ELLs with little confidence in their English skills, he was particularly quiet in whole-group conversation about texts. He was much more likely to be heard speaking softly to his peers in small-group situations. His CELDT score was still at Beginning after 2 years here, at the end of third grade.

José had scored Far Below Basic on the English Language Arts portion of the California Standards Test at the end of third grade, though he would score Proficient (two levels up) at the end of fourth grade, removing some of Ms. Romano's worries about potential remediation. He told me he was "a little bit good" at English and reading, yet thought he was "bad" on his reading benchmarks because of his progress relative to other children's in the class. Indeed, his reading benchmark scores were one of the main causes of worry for Ms. Romano. He had come into her class with a Middle of First Grade score and had made a year and a half's worth of progress on the benchmarks—initially with Ms. Romano's help, as noted in Chapter 2—to pass the "End of Second Grade" benchmark. So, although he and Carlos had both scored Proficient (level 4 of 5) on the CST, his reading benchmark scores would put him at risk of retention in fifth grade, unless he passed the End Of Third Grade test, the retention cutoff, by the end of his fifth grade year.

A closer look at José's test results reveals some complications engendered by setting cutoff scores, or cutscores, on standardized tests. His rapid progress on the English-language CST from Far Below Basic up two levels to Basic is less dramatic when one looks at the numbers associated with test CST score levels. At the time of this writing, an individual student could score up to 600 points on the California Standards Test; the state divides scores into fifths and labels each fifth and each student who scores within that fifth as: 150–268 = Far Below Basic; 269–299 = Below Basic; 300–349 = Basic; 350–392 = Proficient; and 393–600 = Advanced Proficient. (Note the large numerical span included in Advanced Proficient—more than 200 points.) José scored 258 (nearly at the top of the Far Below Basic spread) at the end of third grade, and 313 at the end of fourth grade—a change of 55 points. While this progress is significant, it is more dramatic, and more positive, to describe it as a change of two score levels.

States specify the cutoffs for each proficiency level—i.e., the thresholds for passing. States can also change cutscores, particularly if students do not seem to be making enough progress according to NCLB accountability measures (see Bandeira de Mello, Blankenship, & McLaughlin, 2009; Dillon, 2009). In the past, some states went so far as to exclude ELLs' scores on English-language standardized tests entirely—often unbeknownst to teachers—to avoid having to account for failing scores (Schemo & Fessenden, 2003; Wright, 2006). Recent newspaper stories (Urbina, 2010) have shown that the state boards of education in Alabama, Arizona, Washington, and New York, among others, lowered their cutoff scores or standards when they projected that not enough students would pass their high school exit exams (cf. Warren & Grodsky, 2009). Teachers do receive students' raw numerical scores, but it is much easier to read the labels that come with the scores, and sort students by label, without looking too far into cutscores.

These complications contributed to the stressful situation surrounding José's progress. Until his test scores came back as Proficient on the CST, José was also at risk of being referred to special education (Artiles, Rueda, Salazar, & Higareda, 2005; see also Garcia & Cuéllar, 2006). His English was slow to come, and while he was sensible and clear enough when he spoke, his slow progress prior to the fourth grade meant that several teachers had tried to have him tested for speech delays and learning disabilities. If Ms. Romano had wanted to refer him for special education testing—which she did not because he was making some progress under her tutelage—the school would have had to adhere to certain requirements to make sure they did not violate the Equal Educational Opportunities Act (EEOA), which protects English language learners from linguistic discrimination (Welner, 2004). The school would have had to evaluate him in Spanish and in English, and would have had to make sure the person evaluating him was knowledgeable about second language and literacy acquisition—an unlikely possibility (Welner, 2004).

Poorer children, especially ELLs like José who come from socioeconomically disadvantaged situations, are at higher risk of being identified as learning-disabled. Children in English immersion classrooms are also at risk for identification (Artiles, Klingner, Sullivan, & Fierros, 2010). In their analysis of data from two California districts, Artiles, Rueda, Salazar, and Higareda (2005) found that English language learners in immersion classrooms with little to no primary language support "were more likely to be placed in special education programs than ELLs placed in other language support programs" (p. 296). Indeed, Artiles, Klingner, Sullivan, and Fierros (2010) argue that restrictive language policies in California and Arizona may be causing the large increases in the number of English language learners enrolled in special education programs that they have recently observed. These complexities made José's test scores particularly fraught.

English Only with ELL Writing Errors: Nicole

Nicole was born in the United States to one U.S.-born and one immigrant Latino parent, and had been registered by her mother as an English Only student on the Home Language Survey. On the survey in use in California, when a parent signs a child up for school, the parent self-reports the "language of the home".[7] If they write down a language other than English, their child is immediately signed up to take the California English Language Development Test. If parents are savvy, like Nicole's, they write English as the home language—regardless of what they actually speak at home—and their child avoids the extensive testing and potential discrimination associated with the ELL label. Nicole had receptive Spanish skills, but she could produce very little spoken Spanish and, like Teresa, Carlos, and José, had no Spanish literacy skills.

Nicole's California Standards Test score was Basic (level 3 of 5) at the end of third grade and had moved up to Proficient at the end of fourth, which made her the highest-scoring English Only student in the class. She came in half a year behind on the reading benchmarks, at Middle of Third Grade, and made some, but arguably not enough, progress on them, leaving at the Middle of Fourth Grade. The real dilemma Nicole posed to her teacher was in her English literacy skills. It was not that she exhibited behaviors of reluctant ELL writers such as not writing anything, not knowing what to write about, or copying instead of writing original ideas (Samway & Taylor, 2008); indeed, she had many ideas and could produce written text quite quickly in response to a teacher prompt. Her stamina writing exercise reproduced in Chapter 3, for example, showed her capable of writing 26 words per minute, compared to the more average 14, 15, and 16 words of other students. The problem was that her writing included developmental errors consistent with those of an advanced English language learner, not a native speaker.

One common suggestion to help ELLs improve their writing skills was actually part of the Open Court curriculum: Organize learning around units of study. Ms. Romano also had students use one of the ubiquitous Thinking Maps before they wrote, another recommended strategy.[8] For example, after reading a story called "Food from the 'Hood: A Garden of Hope" (Brill, 2005), Ms. Romano had students write the sequence of the story's events into a flow map, one of the eight Thinking Maps. To make the map, students drew a series of boxes, connected one after the other by arrows, to show the sequence of events in the story. Here is Nicole's sequence:

In Los Angles, CA. In May 1992 Riots destroy the neighborhood some people talk about how to ReBuil their community

Ms. Bird's students decided that planting was more important
restoring to the students plant and Adults work with the students to
Rebuild the town
They disided to make a little buissnes to vote the teenageers soon
realized the students needit more than food to survive shop some
Adult suggested tat the garden come to that kind of Besniss
They planed what's the name of this Busniss
They planed what's the name at this busness [yes, twice, different
second time]
Ms. Bird chosies to name the Busniss the class voted food from the hood
They gave vengetables to sell and help out or pay for college
Ms. Bird's class mixing Igreatinst [ingredients] for right balince and
food. and Helthy
There was a vistor to try's dad and the easy St gave $50,000
Most money went manking salid dressing the students wanted to work
in more area were poor live. Some people work in the garden.

Hers is an incomplete rendering of the story, to say the least. The factual
inaccuracies are less troubling than her errors in spelling, grammar, punctuation, and capitalization. In turn, those are less troubling than Nicole's
apparent lack of attention to producing comprehensible text. This is partly
due to the nature of this particular Thinking Map itself (in this case a flow
map), which is meant to help students sequence events but which leads,
usually, to copying of seemingly key bits of information from the text in
order. There is not a lot of room for imaginative, creative writing, much less
for individuals' responses to the text, when the actual assignment results in
simply filling in the blanks on the hand-drawn map.

What did Nicole's writing look like when she was asked to answer questions about a text? A good example is the story *Toto* (Moskin, 1971), about
a timid boy named Suku, from Unit 1, Risks and Consequences. As noted in
Chapter 3, students had to copy down the Open Court questions and then
write their answers into the reading response journals. Nicole underlined
her answers (and closed the latter two with periods).

1. What risk did toto take by leaving the herd to follow the moon?
    Toto took bravery to leave the herb
2. Why did Suku decide to walk into the bush after freeing toto from
    the trap? Because he stop and he saw a lion and he stand back
3. What risk did toto take to save himself and Suku from the lion?
    What risk is that toto put up his ears and he's trunk and made
    noise.

4. How is this story similar to "Mrs. Frisby and the Crow?"
   <u>Because Mrs. Frisby saved the row and the crow saved Mrs.</u>
   <u>Frisby. Suku saved toto and toto, saved him.</u>

Nicole had the basic facts down—as she should. The class had discussed the story before and after they read it, going over these very questions. Her verb tense confusion ("he stop" and "he stand back"), incorrect usage ("took bravery"), and many other errors indicate the writing patterns of an Advanced, or perhaps Early Advanced, English language learner. I have already lamented the lack of time for writing instruction in the Open Court classroom, but these points bear reiterating. As an English Only student with this level of writing skill, Nicole, as well as her peers, would benefit from time to write for meaningful purposes, being able to brainstorm, outline, revise, share, edit, publish—all parts of the writing process that are seldom granted space in the structured curriculum classroom (Diaz-Rico & Weed, 2006). Indeed, many elements of the writer's workshop—writing in students' native language(s), focusing on collaborative writing, practicing shared writing, providing a range of writing materials, and publishing students' writing (Atwell, 1998; Nation, 2009; Samway, 2006; Samway & Taylor, 2008)—could have been used to improve students' writing in this classroom.

The larger issue Nicole's case brings up is what teachers and administrators ought to do with students labeled as native speakers or English Only who have access to two or more languages at home and who may exhibit oral and written English more characteristic of ELLs. Nicole was capable enough in the classroom to pass for English fluent (Monzó & Rueda, 2009) in conversation, if not in writing. Her EO designation meant that no one needed to worry about her progress on the CELDT and the length of time it might take to reclassify her. Nicole's specific error patterns were often overlooked in the push to show that ELLs and native speakers alike were progressing. Since she was already an EO, she was not, by definition, in need of extra pedagogical attention—and, as I have tried to show, there was little time for Ms. Romano to examine and address the needs of EOs like Nicole.

English Only, White, and Below Basic: Tara

Though it may seem odd to include a White student in this chapter, Tara's existence contributed to and complicated the classroom experiences of Ms. Romano and her ELLs. Tara was the only White student in this class—indeed, one of about 20 in the whole school of several hundred students—and had a complicated family history of poverty, neglect, and custody battles. Her scores placed her at Below Basic at the end of the third grade, and she came into fourth grade at the End of Second Grade on her reading benchmark. She made 1 year of progress and left fourth grade at the End of Third Grade. Like José, Tara would face retention at the end of fifth grade if she continued to make such slow progress. The errors Tara made in her writing were similar, and in some ways worse, than those made by Nicole. Below are Tara's entries in her flow map for the story "Food from the 'Hood: A Garden of Hope" (Brill, 2005), with her punctuation and spelling intact:

> they wont to help the school because it burded Down in 1992.
> they grow a lot of vegetables & plant for ther school and communtiy.
> thy wonted to make stor oners [owners] to buy Stuff.
> they were thinking of a name for there Bissnes to know what theyre Sellining
> they foted [voted] 72 choces [choices] of food to the 5 remanders in there garden.
> they donated food to the Chelter. They mad also Doll 1000 Doller socherschip [scholarship]
> they did respeds of Dessing of 6 moth of Tatlng
> they donted a van and 50,000 Doller to them
> most of the mony went to make the frest ouch of saled Dressing.
> the homeless the Decarded Danner Sand spice from gocher stors [grocery stores].
> they run other dinners.
> they Brodosed [produced] other vegtlbals and the money they get the buy the Bills.
> They earn 27,000 for Clollge fund.

Tara's sequence of events is based on the same story Nicole wrote about, and it is less comprehensible and more error-ridden than Nicole's. As these examples show, when Thinking Maps like the flow map were extended into further writing activities, they became spaces where *meaning* was not as important as filling space with words. All of Tara's writing exhibited these kinds of errors, though. Her story is made worse by the fact that the strictures of the curriculum and testing regime made Ms. Romano equally unable to serve Tara *and* the ELLs in her charge. The students' heavy workload precluded a lot of social maneuvering in Ms. Romano's classroom; they were often too busy writing and reading and copying to exclude or include peers. In class, although Tara was obviously poor, wore clothes that were not always clean, often had unwashed hair, and exhibited poor social skills, she was still able to work with her peers on assignments. When she had the chance, she partnered with Monique, the one African American girl in class, or Brian, the one African American boy, or Matthew, the one English language learner who was in the process of receiving a special education label.

I have used Tara's case here to make the point once again that teaching English language learners is much more complex than simply sorting out, and teaching appropriately to, the ELLs and EOs. Tara was neither an English language learner nor a special needs student, but her low scores and limited literacy skills put her at risk for retention, remediation, and eventual dropping out. Her experiences—and samples of her writing—remind us that reductive, teacher-centered curricula are bad for all students, not just English language learners. They also remind us, once more, that poverty is a critical factor in children's scholastic success or failure. Without attention and help, Tara's schooling future is just as bleak as some of her peers'.

OVERARCHING ISSUES AND RECOMMENDATIONS: HOW TO HELP ENGLISH LANGUAGE LEARNERS

It is clear that talking about English language learners as if they were one monolithic group with the same concerns and problems is misleading, if not downright useless, for teachers, administrators, and policy makers. English language learners come from a variety of backgrounds, and a variety of issues, in and out of school, affect their classroom learning. In this chapter, I have explored the most salient and most widely divergent of these issues. To conclude, I address four larger issues that thread through these individual problems, and make some recommendations regarding our approaches to time, testing, immigration, and poverty in (and out of) the classroom.

Time Issues

The first issue here is one of time. It takes time for an English language learner to acquire English, and time is something none of these children had in abundance. Teresa and Carlos were on their way, and might indeed be reclassified as, Fluent English Proficient within a few more years. The longer their reclassification takes, the more likely it is that they will be kept in separate ELD classes for English language learners in middle school (in California, sixth to eighth grade) and will not have access to the more advanced classes like some of their English Only peers (Valenzuela, 1999; Walqui et al., 2010). Time pressures also affected José and Tara. Each of them faced retention, for different reasons, because they were not making enough progress in the right amount of time. Retention has been shown *not* to work to help children succeed in school (Darling-Hammond & Falk, 1999; Guèvremont, Roos, & Brownell, 2007; Roderick & Nagaoka, 2005), and in fact to *increase* the chances that a student will drop out of school (Pedulla et al., 2003). Regardless, the school district's policies required retention, perhaps as a way to show that the district took progress, and its lack, seriously.

One remedy for the time pressures students and teachers face is to release them from some of the pressures altogether, while maintaining accountability for progress. The entire elementary school period could be seen as an English-learning period for the majority of ELLs who arrive in the early grades (Hakuta et al., 2000). The Working Group on ELL Policy (2010) recommends that the revised No Child Left Behind Act (the Elementary and Secondary Education Act) explicitly state the time it takes to become English proficient (4 to 7 years), and suggests that states use that guide to make their own timeframe for ELLs. In this scenario, we could dispense with threats of retention. If an ELL is not making progress, it is up to the school and district to help the student progress by providing additional support in English and/or in content-area knowledge—and students need to be able to access grade-level content. Ideally, they could then be learning content *and* learning English. Students and states should still be held accountable for progress, but the progress should be measured appropriately, and we should replace sanctions with extra support.

Testing Issues

Tests students took to determine the timing of their progression were deeply problematic, as I have shown here and in Chapter 2. Teachers received too much conflicting information, and in turn, students and teachers faced undue pressure to make and show progress on tests that were especially unfair and inaccurate when used with ELLs (Wright, 2006). To make matters worse, states can and do change cutoff scores to make claims about progress that may or may not be correct. In the 2001 NCLB accountability policy, states were neither required nor authorized to use other measures of ELL students' progress besides standardized tests. As it stands, then, NCLB has not made life—or success—easier for English language learners (Fusarelli, 2004; Menken, 2006; Wright, 2005).

As of this writing, states are required by Title III of NCLB to identify children who have English language needs, and many states employ home language surveys to do this (Abedi, 2007; Dúran, 2008). However, NCLB does not specify methods of identification, and there is no nationally recognized survey or identification tool. To make matters more confusing, recent research suggests that home language surveys lack validity as initial identifying instruments due to a variety of factors (Bailey & Kelly, 2010). Many researchers suggest that ELLs' native language knowledge should be assessed at the same time (cf. Echevarria & Graves, 2003) to provide additional valuable information to students' teachers about their abilities in their first language; but the pressure to categorize and advance ELLs often leaves first language skills at the wayside.

The first solution is to revisit the English-language instruments we as a nation use to assess ELLs' progress in English. English language learners do need to be tested in English, to measure both their rate of English acquisition (oral and written) and their content-area knowledge, at least insofar as they can display such knowledge in English. The California English Language Development Test in California attempts to measure the first part—rate of English acquisition. However, it is a test of controlled language production, in an assessment environment, and it does not give a sense of what students can do with English in nontesting settings (Ellis, 2008). One solution to this incompleteness would be to require teachers to make informal assessments of students' oral and written English in the classroom at least twice a year. Such informal assessments of language in use would complement the CELDT and would ameliorate the time delays of it. Teachers ought to know what their students are capable of doing in the present, not what they were capable of doing when the CELDT test was administered, which is often months before the scores come to the classroom (Walqui et al., 2010; see also Menken, 2008). Standardizing these informal assessments would require that teachers knew enough English language development and acquisition patterns to make sense of the results. Such knowledge ought to be imparted and practiced in teacher education programs, where teacher candidates need to be armed with as much information about English language acquisition as possible.

Immigration Issues

As many scholars before me have made clear, the effects of immigration (of parents and/or children) on students' scholastic performance are numerous.[9] Most of the children I have described here, and many of their peers, were transnationalized by immigration. Either they had personally immigrated, often with only one parent, or their parents had immigrated at some point in their lives and they had been born here. In either case (except for Tara), family members and ways of life were left behind, and children—and their parents—had to adapt while trying to learn a new language and new ways of being in the world (cf. Portes & Rumbaut, 2006).

Stresses of immigration—the sudden absence of networks of support, family members, friends, and familiar places—are intensified for those who come to the United States illegally. Current global trends in both the rate and kinds of human migration show that the United States will only see an increase in unauthorized entrants with low educational levels and few resources on which to draw (Capps et al., 2005; Passel, 2005). Approximately 2 million of the 11.9 million unauthorized immigrants to the United States are children (as of March 2008) (Passel & Cohn, 2008). Unauthorized immigrants are less likely to ask for help or advice from their teachers and school officials (Morse & Ludovina, 1999), and are less likely to receive adequate health care services (Capps, Ku, Fix, Furgiuele, Passel, Ramchand, McNiven, & Perez-Lopez, 2002; Passel, 2005). At the same time, their children are more at risk for educational problems (García & Cuéllar, 2006; Suárez-Orozco, Suárez-Orozco, & Todorova, 2008; Valdés, 2001; Valenzuela, 1999,) and more likely to have suffered physical or emotional trauma as part of their immigration experience (Nazario, 2007; Suárez-Orozco, 2005). Because they and their parents are an invisible and vulnerable minority, often living in fear of exposure, we know relatively little about such children's school experiences, and less about how school successes may lead to less risky life situations.

In the United States, one of the fundamental—if sometimes problematic—goals (Gibson, Gándara, & Koyama, 2004; Suárez-Orozco, 2005) of public schools is to assimilate immigrants into American life and construct American citizens (Olsen, 1997; Salomone, 2010; Tyack, 2003). This socialization project is complicated by the existence of undocumented students—how do schools turn those who are not on the pathway to legal citizenship into American citizens? In their analysis of the Harvard Immigration Project data, the Suárez-Orozcos (2002; also with Todorova, 2008) argue that to increase the chances of success for unauthorized children, we must design educational policies so that they "will one day be able to better themselves and contribute to their new society" (2008, p. 375).[10] Chavez (1991) has studied the family and work lives of undocumented immigrants from an anthropological perspective, and similarly urges U.S. society to imagine "undocumented immigrants as part of the community" (p. 186). Legal protections for undocumented children and youth seem necessary to make such contributions and community-building possible.

Other suggestions to support immigrant youth include encouraging, or even requiring, bilingualism in programs, practices, and assessments. One way to do this at the federal level would be to allow and encourage states to develop assessment and accountability systems for students learning in two or more languages to foster bilingualism and combat language loss

(Working Group on ELL Policy, 2010). Dual-language programs, in which children may enter speaking only one language, but exit speaking, reading, and writing in two, foster positive self-identities in addition to their numerous academic benefits (Linton & Franklin, 2010; Morales & Aldana, 2010). Such programs should be considered and bolstered to help integrate the strengths of immigrant children—be they of Latino or other descent—into mainstream curriculum and assessment systems.

Poverty Issues

So many of Ms. Romano's students were in the NCLB low socioeconomic subgroup that discussions of the effects of poverty on test scores and school performance make little sense at the classroom level. Numerous studies have shown the deleterious effects of early childhood poverty on school performance in general[11] and on immigrant children's life chances in particular.[12] To make matters worse, it "appears certain that SES [socioeconomic status] is powerful in predicting rate of English acquisition" (Hakuta, Butler, & Witt, 2000, p. 13). The poverty statistics at a school like Laurel Elementary often mean that children are in two or more subgroups: English language learners, low socioeconomic status, Hispanic/Latino (sometimes), and, occasionally, Special Education.

Because children who live in poverty are often concentrated in poorer neighborhoods and schools within those neighborhoods (Berliner, 2006), a school like Laurel shoulders greater accountability burdens than nearby schools with fewer ELLs or fewer students in the low socioeconomic subgroup. At the moment, NCLB requires schools to be accountable for raising achievement of all subgroups, but does not take into account the extra pressures on schools with higher populations of subgroups with traditionally lower scores. It is possible that future revisions to NCLB/ESEA might take school contexts into account, and might change Title I funding requirements to show awareness of these densely grouped, higher-need populations. One measure that has been shown to increase the school success of socioeconomically disadvantaged children is preschool (Campbell, Ramey, Pungello, Sparling, & Miller-Johnson, 2002; Haskins & Rouse, 2005; Suárez-Orozco & Suárez-Orozco, 2009; Takanishi, 2004).

One way to positively affect the schooling experiences of poor children is to turn schools that serve them into community schools, so that they become sites around which community partners—i.e., health, dentistry, and vision clinics—make a coordinated effort to meet the needs of their students, families, and communities in and out of school (Blank, Jacobson, & Pearson, 2009). National nonprofit organizations like Communities in

Schools (www.cisnet.org) organize and maintain health, social services, and academic support for children in schools, creating a safety net for students where none had been available before (Dubin, 2009). There are many successful models for such approaches (Blank et al., 2009), though most rely on external funding that waxes and wanes. One way to support students of low socioeconomic status in schools would be to standardize funding mechanisms for such programs; schools could create their own models, according to their community's specific needs, with guaranteed federal financial support. The NCLB/ESEA reauthorization is a chance to make preschool more accessible to the populations who need it most, and make community school funding more stable, although the chances of these changes happening, given the current makeup of the Congress and the country's current financial situation, are admittedly low.

If we know that English language learners are so poorly served by structured curriculum, and so inhibited and constrained by high-stakes standardized testing regimes, as I have shown in this book so far, the next logical question is: How are we helping teachers develop skills and dispositions for teaching in these contexts? In the next chapter, I look at the training and testing of teacher candidates in current programs.

CHAPTER 5

Learning to Teach in the Age of Accountability

A year after I collected data in Ms. Romano's room, she and I had lunch together. She had known, she said, that this book would not portray her teaching in the best light, although that was not my intention. The year I observed had been a bad one. She had had a lot of students with low scores, and faced constant pressure to adhere to the curriculum and help students perform well on tests. I asked her how new teachers—who are increasingly evaluated via performance assessments before they receive their credentials—handle the standardized testing regimes in place in schools like Laurel Elementary. I wanted to know if she felt that new teachers could resist testing mandates and pressures. As a cautionary tale, she told me the story of her own attempt to stand up to testing.

In the school year after I left her classroom, the district adopted a new set of tests linked directly to the state's content area standards. The district's thrice-annual tests conveniently mirrored the content of the California Standards Test, and teachers were meant to teach to them, not to "teach to the test" but to teach the right content at the right time, a slippery distinction in practice, Ms. Romano found. She took a stand: She decided *not* to teach to the test in the mandated way; instead, she did what she thought she ought to do, teaching content in the order that she and her students found interesting, implementing alternative activities like literature circles, guided reading, and science units. At the end of the year, three negative events convinced her to go along with the school's test-focused curriculum.

At the thrice-yearly schoolwide assemblies, when students got awards for passing their midyear assessments (the ones she had refused to teach to), most of her students were passed over. She had not taught the content at the right time, and so her students had failed the district's standards-based tests. Second, in a special meeting, the principal made it clear to her that future evaluations of her teaching would focus on whether she was teaching the appropriate content in the right sequence (to align with the district's tests). If she wanted a positive evaluation, the principal suggested, she might want to fall into line. Third, and most troublesome of all, because fourth-grade CST scores determine students' placements, some of her students' scores were not high enough to get them into the middle schools they wanted to get into. The next year, she was back to teaching to the test. Within a year, the assessment regime at Laurel and in her district had convinced Ms. Romano of the futility of fighting the pressures of assessment and accountability in her classroom.

We are in the midst of extreme accountability pressures; teachers, teacher candidates, professors, credential programs, and colleges of education are increasingly evaluated and measured by various external bodies (Rinke & Valli, 2010; Snyder, 2009) with a vigor and frequency that are unprecedented. In this chapter, I focus on the conundrum facing present and future teachers in this environment.

PREPARING TEACHER CANDIDATES TO TEACH ELLs IN THE AGE OF ACCOUNTABILITY

The overarching goal of credentialing programs, from the 4-year undergraduate variety to alternative certification models, is to arm teachers with the skills, knowledge, and dispositions (Damon, 1995) they will need as they embark on their teaching careers. Programs align their offerings with their state's standards and requirements, because states, not programs, grant credentials. Credentialing bodies—composed of teachers, administrators, teacher educators, and sometimes community businesspeople—often use their power to force changes in teacher education program content. One major way they do this is by making assessment drive instruction, on a large scale.

Take the outcomes of the State of California's Special Education Reading Task Force, convened in 1996, as an example. The Task Force conducted 3 years of research, and published the California Reading Initiative in conjunction with the State Department of Education and the State Board of Education (Special Education Reading Task Force, California Department of Education, & California State Board of Education, 1999). The Initiative included new English-language arts content standards and a new framework for language arts skills. In order to ensure that teacher credential programs reorganized their content to align with the new content standards and framework, the initiative's contents were used to create the Reading Instruction Competence Assessment (RICA®, Pearson Education, Inc.). The RICA is a test of specific "tasks, knowledge, and abilities related to effective reading instruction" (Overview of the RICA, para. 4, http://www.rica.nesinc. com/RC14_overview.asp) that all elementary teacher candidates must pass before entering the classroom. The test was mandated by the CDE to ensure that credential programs changed their course offerings in the language arts as needed to teach the content on the RICA test. As a result, when California's teachers go into the field with their RICA certification, we know that they are armed, on paper at least, with knowledge about how to qualitatively assess students' literacy development, skills, and needs.

When these RICA-approved new teachers enter the classroom, the first problem they encounter may well be with the structured language arts curriculum used in the district in which they are hired. As I discussed in Chapter 3, such curricular implementations often leave teachers little space to address the needs of ELLs. Some suggest that new teachers may find comfort in structured programs, because they offer a set pathway to follow. But for seasoned teachers, this is not always the case. Lee, Ajayi, and Richards (2007) found that the longer teachers had been teaching—without or with Open Court—the less satisfied they were with its utility for ELLs. Overall, the majority of teachers surveyed felt that Open Court was "generally ineffective" with English language learners (p. 31), and to the extent that we understand teachers' implementations of these curricula, we might imagine that their dissatisfaction influenced their use of it with ELLs in some way. There is little research on what teachers actually do with these programs when no one is surveilling them, so it is hard to say how teachers may make modifications to structured programs for ELLs. Based on the percentages of passing RICA scores, and now percentages of passing scores on the teacher performance assessments, we do know that teachers leave credential programs knowing, theoretically, many ways to effectively teach and assess. We also know that when they get into the classroom, they are often forced to teach using curricula that they did not design and that they do not necessarily find useful for their ELL students.[1]

Teachers of English language learners feel particularly pressured in environments with high-stakes testing regimes and structured language arts curricula (Wright, 2005). This is worth emphasizing, because it is estimated that within a few years something like one in every four students will be classified as an English language learner in California's classrooms. This pressure results in changes to teaching, assessment, and learning, as I reported in Chapters 2 and 3. In their national survey of teacher beliefs and practices around high-stakes testing, Pedulla et al. (2003) found that 90% of teachers believed that their state test "inaccurately measures student achievement for English as a second language students" (p. 45), and "does not accurately measure what students who are acquiring English as a second language know and can do" (p. 42). Powers (2010) found that NCLB's assessment pressures and testing mandates forced urban teachers to narrow their instructional content, and led to the use of fewer engaging strategies in the classroom. To make matters worse, teachers in schools with higher percentages of low-socioeconomic status students were impacted to a greater degree. When teachers of ELLs do not believe in the accuracy of their students' standardized test scores, and when pressure to make progress forces teachers to narrow their curricula, teacher anxiety increases.

Pennington (2004) argues that our national obsession with accountability, with its monolithic definitions of literacy and focus on *training* teachers instead of educating them, has colonized literacy education. She saw it happen at the elementary school in which she taught in Austin, Texas, for 14 years, from 1987 to 2001. She watched the teaching and testing of ELLs change as the school went from being a place with a rich, student-centered curriculum where children generally passed the state test, to a school focused on students' test scores on the high-stakes Texas Assessment of Academic Skills (TAAS, used from 1991 to 2002, replaced with the Texas Assessment of Knowledge and Skills [TAKS]). The corresponding lack of teacher initiative and professionalism, and narrowing of the curriculum for English language learners that Pennington reports, are a cautionary tale. Valli et al. (2008) report similar results from their study of teaching and administrative changes at four elementary schools in the wake of NCLB's accountability policies. Agee (2004) and Ruiz and Morales-Ellis (2005) have shown how teachers' identities as professionals are negatively impacted by curricular mandates, particularly in high-stakes settings.

The gross discrepancies between teaching preparation ideals and classroom realities do not end with pedagogical changes. Indeed, they are amplified by the discrepancies between the ways we assess teachers' preparedness to teach in credential programs, via performance assessments, and the ways they may well be assessed in the field, via their students' standardized test score growth, or the "value" they "add" to their students' test scores. I look next at performance assessments, and in the following section I discuss the growing movement to define teacher effectiveness by, and base job security on, the value they add to their students' standardized test scores.

ASSESSING TEACHER CANDIDATES

Teacher candidates—those taking coursework to complete a teaching credential—are no strangers to standardized tests. Take California, where candidates must pass the California Basic Educational Skills Test (CBEST), the California Subject Examinations for Teachers (CSET) for elementary teachers (or the Single Subject Assessments for Teaching [SSAT] for middle and high school teachers), and the Reading Instruction Competence Assessment. If they graduated from high school after 2006, they will have also passed the California High School Exit Exam (CAHSEE). This list is not even accounting for the annual standardized tests they took as children.

In an effort to assess future teachers' performance as teachers, the field is turning away from these kinds of paper-and-pencil tests toward performance assessments. This increasing use of performance assessments exemplifies the diverging paths of teacher preparation programs on the one hand, and the high-stakes assessment world of the K-12 classroom on the other.

Performance Assessments

Performance assessments can accomplish many tasks. Most importantly, they assess individuals' ability to teach. The data they provide can be used to evaluate and improve credential programs (Peck et al., 2010). In addition, the experience of engaging in them can provide feedback to teacher candidates about how to teach (Snyder, 2009). One of the potentially useful components of performance assessments is their utility for program faculty in revising course content for credential students to address their needs. For instance, when the California State University, Fresno faculty found that their students were not performing well in terms of meeting the needs of English language learners according to their site supervisors on a CSU systemwide exit survey, they made changes to their program at various levels, and then tracked students' scores on the parts of the Fresno Assessment of Student Teachers (FAST) assessment that focus on ELLs. They were able to document "improved candidate knowledge and practice in teaching ELL" students (Torgerson, Macy, Beare, & Tanner, 2009, p. 80; see also Bunch, Aguirre, & Téllez, 2009), and they credit students' increased preparation to their efforts to change their own program. Some research has begun to show that teachers with positive scores on performance assessments can have a positive influence on their students' achievement on standardized test scores (Milanowski, Kimball, & White, 2004).

California's performance assessments are worth some scrutiny because, as of this writing, the Performance Assessment of California Teachers (PACT) is being piloted by 15 more states and 30 more schools of education as part of a national teacher performance assessment (Darling-Hammond, 2010a).[2] Initially mandated in California in 1998 by the passage of Senate Bill 2042 (Senate Bill 2042, 1998), performance assessment was delayed because of financial constraints until the passage of Senate Bill 1209 (Senate Bill 1209, 2006), which required teacher candidates who entered programs after July 1, 2008, to pass the TPA or PACT. The state currently recognizes three different assessments: the PACT; the California Teacher Performance Assessment (CalTPA); and the Fresno Assessment of Student Teachers (FAST), for use only at CSU Fresno (Torgerson et al., 2009). Because these are performance assessments, parts or all of them (depending on the assessment) are completed during student teaching, when candidates have real students with whom to work (Chung, 2008). Each requires prospective teachers to plan lessons, specify adaptations for English language learners and students with special needs, and analyze and reflect on their teaching. The CalTPA and PACT require videotaping of instruction to support analyses and reflections; all three ask candidates to articulate what they will do in the future based on their own assessment of their teaching and students' learning. The pieces of these assessments align with the 13 Teacher Performance Expectations adopted by the California Commission on Teacher Credentialing (2001; see also Chung, 2008). Like the RICA, these performance assessments force programs to change their content to align with and teach to the Teacher Performance Expectations.

Implementation of Performance Assessments

There have been problems with the implementation of the TPAs, as they are referred to in the California State University system where I work (and score TPAs). University administrators have struggled with a lack of financial resources to support staffing, as they decide who teaches teacher candidates how to complete the TPAs, in what courses, and how long it takes to embed and then teach them.[3] They struggle with scoring, because there are four TPAs, and each one takes at least an hour to score—at a campus with 500 candidates, that is 2,000 hours of scoring, plus more time for students who fail on their first try and need remediation and further scoring. Then there are the costs of remediation itself; programs may create special courses to help their students pass on the second attempt. Finally, there is the issue of technological support for the TPAs in the form of data systems paid for by universities *and* candidates that universities use to manage and score the assessments, and video cameras and related equipment needed to help candidates videotape themselves. Some campuses hire TPA coordinators and pay instructors and scorers, if necessary (Guaglianone, Payne, Kinsey, & Chiero, 2009); private institutions are also able to charge their students extra fees to cover some costs.

Another problem with the implementation of performance assessments is initial resistance on the part of university instructors to what they sometimes see as yet another top-down mandate for program change (Kornfeld, Grady, Marker, & Ruddell, 2007). As the full picture of the purpose of performance assessments emerges, and their benefits to programs and students are more clear, *and* as administrators work with faculty to share and reduce the burdens of adding performance assessments to courses and scoring performance assessments, this resistance might be expected to fade. The same can be said for teacher candidates themselves, who complain about the time involved in completing and turning in the performance assessments, even as they recognize the value of the reflective self-assessment they engender (Okhremtchouk et al., 2009). Little research has yet been done on issues of remediation for the CalTPA and PACT. Since candidates admitted to credential programs after July 1, 2008, are not eligible to receive teaching credentials in California unless they pass their institution's performance assessment, programs have tried to help those who fail by providing additional courses and fees. The wisdom of such measures and the benefits of remediation to candidates and to the profession are as yet unclear.

Future of Performance Assessments

Proponents of performance assessments argue that the move toward them may be useful, especially if it is coupled with changes to teacher education such as mandatory accreditation of credential programs and extensive clinical experience with mentor teachers (Darling-Hammond, 2010a). Darling-Hammond often uses the transformation of medical schools from unregulated programs to more uniform, high-standards bodies with mandatory teaching hospitals and required courses as examples of the ways standardization and accreditation could help strengthen teacher education. At the moment, however, what we teach in the best teacher education programs does not match up with the actual environments teachers encounter. To understand the depth of the disparities between training and practice, we can return to the medical school analogy.

Imagine if newly minted M.D.s were told that their success in patient treatment was going to be measured solely by patients' lab test results, and not also by more holistic evaluations of patient health. Imagine if they were told that they must evaluate all patients using similar sets of exams, even if they had been trained to differentiate exams depending on the needs of the patient. To take the analogy one step further, imagine if, upon leaving their residency programs, instead of being able to rely on the knowledge they gained through extensive coursework and clinical training, they were told that they had to follow directions in a textbook or in a how-to video for each procedure, because their supervisors were not sure they were capable of doing it themselves.

This example reflects the disparities between preparation and practice that new teachers face because the movement to assess teacher candidates via their performance has not made it from the credential program to the K-12 classroom, where test scores are increasingly used as measures of student learning and therefore success. English language learners are arguably the population most vulnerable, and with the most to lose, in the change to judging teacher effectiveness by their students' test scores—the "value-added" approach, which I discuss in the next section.

TEACHING IN A VALUE-ADDED WORLD

In the summer of 2010, reporters from the *Los Angeles Times* printed the newspaper's analysis of 7 years of standardized test data from the Los Angeles Unified School District. This value-added approach (Buddin, 2010; Felch, Song, & Smith, 2010) was meant to show the "effectiveness" of public school teachers. According to its proponents, value-added analysis of students' test scores "offers the closest thing available to an objective assessment of teachers" (Felch, Song, & Smith, 2010). To conduct the analysis, a student's past performance on tests was used to project his or her future scores. The difference between the statistical prediction and the student's actual performance after a year is supposed to represent the "value" that the teacher has added or subtracted. The results are—of course—partly related to other issues in a child's life (Baker et al., 2010), but the claim is that, over time and with data on at least 60 students, the statistics for each teacher are "reliable" indicators of their teaching effectiveness (as measured by student test score improvement). As an example of such effectiveness, the *Los Angeles Times* article highlights an "effective teacher," Miguel Aguilar, whose fifth-grade students were in the 34th percentile compared to other children in the Los Angeles Unified School District when they came into his class, and left it in the 61st percentile.

Value-Added Measurement Linked to Merit Pay

The results of publicizing test scores by teacher name in Los Angeles are for now mostly unknown,[4] but student scores are being linked to teacher job security and even remuneration in different ways across the United States. In the Pittsburgh Public Schools district, for instance, the school board and union recently agreed to begin performance pay for teachers (Rujumba, 2010), linked to an as-yet-uncrafted evaluation model that will doubtless include some form of value-added analysis. Bill Gates has recently invested

$335 million dollars in a large-scale experiment to link student achieve-ment, measured by value-added models, to teacher practices as seen in video evaluations of their teachers (Dillon, 2010). Michelle Rhee, former Chancel-lor of the Washington, D.C. schools, got the D.C. teachers' union to agree to a contract in which value-added analyses comprise up to 50% of the weight of teacher effectiveness assessments (District of Columbia Public Schools, 2010; Turque, 2009, 2010 [see also the film *Waiting for Superman*]). The U.S. Department of Education is behind this movement; Arne Duncan, the current U.S. Secretary of Education, began such a system during his ten-ure as superintendent of the Chicago Public Schools (Duncan, 2009). States who wish to apply for Race to the Top funds (over 40 million available dollars) must outline and follow a process similar to the one that Rhee had already begun (U.S. Department of Education, 2010).

In the D.C. Public Schools model, named IMPACT, teachers are evalu-ated based on five components (District of Columbia Public Schools, 2010). The first component, Individual Value-Added Student Achievement Data (IVA), based on analyses of student test score improvement data, will count for *half* (50%) of their evaluation. (This is also known as value-added measurement, which I discuss below.) Their performance on a nine-point Teaching and Learning Framework, which will be scored holistically by five different assessors, makes up 35% of their IMPACT score. The next 10% of the evaluation is based on the teacher's Commitment to the School Community, assessed twice a year by their administrator (or program su-pervisor) on a five-point rubric. The last 5% of the score is based on school-wide achievement data, meant to ensure teamwork and a cooperative spirit at each school site. The fifth component, Core Professionalism, does not add to a teacher's score, but instead enables administrators to take away IMPACT points if teachers are found to be "slightly below standard" or "significantly below standard" in the categories of attendance, on-time ar-rival, "policies and procedures," and "respect" (District of Columbia Public Schools, 2010). There are variations for these categories if value-added data cannot be generated for a teacher (in lower grades, for now) or a school for one reason or another. The district continues to revise the evaluation program based on community feedback (2010-2011 was the second year of its implementation).

The main component of the DCPS model, value-added measurement (VAM), is cited by those in favor of merit pay. These plans "realign teach-ing incentives" so that teacher pay is linked with "classroom performance" (Buddin et al., 2007, cited in Buddin, 2010, p. 19), as gauged by VAM. Like the arguments for Scientifically Based Research that I describe in Chapter 3, merit pay advocates deploy terminology that at first hearing is hard to counter. Merit pay systems, they argue, are "results-oriented" because they will produce "specific student outcomes" and thus "reward for better classroom performance" and ultimately give us a "different ordering of teacher effectiveness and improved overall levels of student learning" (p. 19). Results from previous studies of merit pay systems suggest that it works some of the time in some situations (Murnane & Cohen, 1986). In his 2009 address at the Institute of Education Sciences Research Conference, U.S. Secretary of Education Arne Duncan said:

> It's too early to see real results about pay-for-performance initiatives. There aren't a lot of studies showing it boosts student achievement, but there is plenty of evidence that it boosts worker productivity in other industries, so why shouldn't we try it? (p. 5)

Cautions to Consider

Why not, indeed? Well, there are a few reasons we might want to go *very* slowly in our efforts to link teacher pay to students' performance on standardized tests. The first reason is that it is not at all clear that standardized tests are the most reliable measures of *teacher effectiveness* or of *student learning* (Baker et al., 2010), though this movement assumes both statements are true. Making our judgment of teachers' effectiveness based solely, or even partially, on students' test scores means that we accept that test scores are valid measures of learning. A teacher might not be effective at teaching critical thinking, or educating contributing American citizens, or producing productive members of society, but might be able to teach his or her students how to do well on the narrow range of skills that are assessable on standardized tests. At the least, test scores are valid measures of how well children do on tests. This trend is especially problematic for English language learners, since merit pay calculations for teachers will include the scores of ELLs just as they are currently included in NCLB accountability policies and just as they are counted against schools when NCLB-related sanctions are made.

Another result of relying too heavily on value-added measurement systems—and, worse, linking VAM to merit pay—is the potential increase in testing that they will surely produce. In Washington, D.C., for instance, the standardized test was once given to students in the third grade and up, leaving kindergarteners and first and second graders free from the developmentally inappropriate burdens of high-stakes testing pressures. With the advent of IMPACT, however, the D.C. Public Schools system is designing and implementing "developmentally appropriate standardized tests" for those students—3 more years' worth of tests in children's lives, so that their teachers can be judged based on the tests. It is not clear that developmentally appropriate paper-and-pencil standardized tests even exist for such young children, and now they will be required to take them. Their teachers will be paid more or less, and retained or fired, based partly on their 5-year-old students' standardized test scores.

A corollary to an increase in testing is an indubitable increase in test preparation, test pressure, and teaching to the test that will occur in places where job security is linked to test score performance. Once teachers accept that their students' test scores will be used to evaluate them and to determine whether or not they can keep their jobs, there will be a strong incentive to teach to the test (see again Baker et al., 2010). Because states' standardized tests are usually linked to the state's content-area standards, we may hear a lot about how teachers are teaching to the standards, not the test. But if, for example, content-area standards include art and social studies, and the test focuses only on English language arts and math, there is little doubt teachers will most likely feel pressure to leave art and social studies by the wayside. Administrators will aid in this endeavor, either knowingly or unwittingly, because it is in their best interests to work at high-scoring schools, with high-scoring teachers and students.

The last problem is one of statistics. Statistical pitfalls await those who place too much faith in value-added systems, because small sample sizes mean less reliable data (Baker et al., 2010; Turque, 2009). In addition to sample size problems, the cutscore problem rears its head again—from a new angle, that of gauging improvement. As I showed in Chapter 4, cutscores—the cutoff point on a numerical score scale at which a student has passed a test, often set to indicate different levels (e.g., 150-268 out of 600 = Far Below Basic, 269-299 = Below Basic, etc.)—are problematic (for children and schools) because they are arbitrary, and because they can be manipulated.

Consider the example of Nancy Polachek, a teacher whose principal rated her as one of her top performers (at Third Street Elementary in Hancock Park in Los Angeles). The *Los Angeles Times* reporters write that "the *Times* analysis suggests that the principal is right: Polacheck's students gained 5 percentile points in math after a year in her class, and 4 points in English. That put her in the top 5% of elementary school teachers." Five percentile points of gains does not seem like a lot, but it may well be in the context of Ms. Polacheck's classroom—the numbers are opaque, and leave more questions than they answer. For instance, did all of her students make gains, or did the gains outweigh the losses? Were those 5 percentile points enough to move any of her students from one test level (i.e. Proficient) to another (i.e., Advanced)? What were the other "top 5% of elementary school teachers'" gains, and did any teachers' students make larger gains than 5 percentile points? Why? These are some of the many questions value-added measurements do not address.[5]

These problems are recognized by districts and policy makers, which is why Washington, D.C.'s IMPACT plan, for example, uses other measures of performance to judge teachers. If only 50% of a teacher's evaluation is based on student test score increases, will teachers feel more or less pressure to teach to the test than they already do? The Los Angeles Unified School District plans to base 30% of its evaluations on value-added measures by 2012 if the federal funds are made available to them to do so (Felch et al., 2010). In both cases, we will have to wait and see. As noted, past research (Murnane & Cohen, 1986) suggests that teaching is a complex endeavor ill-suited to performance-based pay situations, despite Duncan's (2009) suggestion that it might work because it "boosts productivity in other industries" (p. 5). Teaching, I would argue, is not just a business, and applying businesslike methods of evaluation to teachers' "productivity" may well worsen our already pressurized system.

As teacher performance assessments are increasingly used across the nation, more and more teacher candidates will have their teaching effectiveness evaluated through their planning of lessons, analyzing their performance, and reflecting on improvement. However, when they get to the classroom, the meaning of the word *performance* will undergo a 180-degree shift, from the plan-teach-analyze-reflect pattern to the concept of value-added student test score analyses. It is likely that everything new teachers will have learned about teaching and assessment in their credential programs will sit, unused, as they implement prepackaged curricula to prepare their students to do well enough on the standardized tests. As for English language learners, they will face increasing pressure to do well on tests and will be the recipients of more test-centered teaching (Baker et al., 2010).

These contrasts are fundamentally a policy problem. As long as the teacher preparation movement and the value-added, test-centered assessment of classroom teaching and learning movement continue on their separate, and disparate, paths, this situation will only get more tangled and complicated for teachers and students.[6] If teacher educators can successfully argue that the potential effectiveness of teachers is "proven" by their results on performance assessments, policies could be implemented that match that belief in practice in the classroom. In the meantime, we need to help present and future teachers of English language learners cope in existing high-stakes contexts. I discuss these more realistic futures in the next two sections.

EDUCATING AND SUPPORTING TEACHERS OF ELLs IN HIGH-STAKES SETTINGS

There is a large body of research about what teachers of English language learners should be educated to know before they enter the classroom. There is also research about what kinds of support existing teachers need in order to best support ELLs, including best practices for professional development.

Teacher Preparation

In 2001, on behalf of the National Clearinghouse for Bilingual Education, Menken and Antunez reviewed data from a survey conducted by the American Association of Colleges for Teacher Education (AACTE) of the ways teacher education programs educated their candidates about English language learners and learning. They used a three-part theoretical framework to assess bilingual and mainstream teacher education programs in the areas of knowledge of pedagogy, linguistics, and cultural and linguistic diversity. Although they were concerned with both bilingual and general education certification programs, I have focused on the ramifications of their findings for general education teachers, three of which are particularly problematic, even 10 years later. First, only one-sixth of the responding programs required preparation for mainstream teachers about the teaching of English language learners. Second, states and programs did not emphasize the necessity and importance of linguistic knowledge for their candidates, and this lack of emphasis was reflected in program offerings. Third, undergraduate programs in particular tended to cover course material about ELLs and multiculturalism in the broad strokes of survey courses, without allowing for enough depth of learning about individual topics.

There have been some positive changes, particularly in the area of additional coursework for future teachers about how to teach English language learners (Lucas, Villegas, & Freedson-Gonzalez, 2008; see also Lucas & Grinberg, 2008). Future improvements for teacher education programs—about which there is much research—can be roughly sorted into four main areas. The first, *teacher knowledge,* encompasses a very broad body of research on the kinds of knowledge teachers should have about how children learn, and how curriculum is connected to the larger social purposes of education, especially for English language learners (Darling-Hammond, 2006; Darling-Hammond & Bransford, 2005; García, Arias, Murri, & Serna, 2010).

The second area, *linguistic knowledge* for teachers of English language learners, includes both the specific content teachers need to know (Lucas et al., 2008; Milk, Mercado, & Sapiens, 1992; Snow & Fillmore, 2000), as well as the time and space they need in credential programs to practice strategies for teaching English language learners (cf. Téllez & Waxman, 2006).

The third term, *community embeddedness*, arises from research on the utility of "situated preparation" of teachers of English language learners within the communities from whence ELLs come (García, Arias, Murri, & Serna, 2010). Such programs can foster "the development of teacher knowledge of the dynamics of language in children's lives and communities" (p. 132). At the very least, teacher candidates need access to, and sustained contact with, the children and parents in the communities they will serve. Such contact should be grounded in and guided by culturally responsive teaching practices. These experiences enable teacher candidates to learn about the linguistic and cultural repertoires of their students while learning how to bring those strengths into their future classrooms (Gay, 2000; Weinstein, Taumlinson-Clarke, & Curran, 2004).

Teacher dispositions are the fourth main area of growing interest and research: what teachers ought to understand about how their own beliefs might influence their treatment, and teaching, of students who are different from them in some way. The current thinking about dispositions suggests that programs should require their teacher candidates to explore their beliefs, identities, and cultural heritages (García et al., 2010) so that they will be more disposed to build on the strengths ELLs bring to the classroom. This perspective is reflected in official documents like California's Teacher Performance Expectations (California Commission on Teacher Credentialing, 2001), whose contents are linked to the TPA and PACT assessments, which explicitly require teachers to be able to "promote student effort and engagement and create a positive climate for learning," and "establish rapport with all students and their families for supporting academic and personal success through caring, respect, and fairness" (p. A-15). Furthermore, teacher "candidates respond appropriately to sensitive issues and classroom discussions" and "are aware of their own personal values and biases and recognize ways in which these values and biases affect the teaching and learning of students. They resist racism and acts of intolerance" (p. A-15).

Positive teacher dispositions toward ELLs' linguistic abilities should be cultivated, but they are only a means to an end. As Milk, Mercado, and Sapiens (1992) argue, the ultimate task of teacher preparation programs is to:

> help teachers learn to create challenging learning environments for language minority students. Emphasis should be on practice and assumptions underlying that practice, not on discrete skills. This calls for programs that

promote teachers who reflect on what they do in the classroom and on how
this affects language minority students and second language learners. (p. 9)

While teacher preparation programs align their content with performance assessments, program content itself should be shifted to address the
four domains previously noted. Program faculty ought to incorporate recent work on teacher knowledge; augment or add coursework on linguistic
knowledge in theory and practice (Lucas et al., 2008); attempt to situate
their programs in communities with linguistically diverse populations; and
cultivate teachers who are positively disposed toward English language
learners. These changes are not easily or quickly done, but they can be made
over time. The goal is to make sure that teachers of ELLs reflect on their
own classroom practices and understand how their actions affect the learning their students are able to undertake (Milk et al., 1992). A concomitant
goal is to make sure teachers are prepared, upon exiting their programs, to
be the most effective teachers they can be for English language learners in
high-stakes settings.

Teacher Support

The needs of existing teachers of English language learners are somewhat different, as indicated by a survey conducted by Gándara, Maxwell-
Jolly, and Driscoll (2005) of teachers in 22 California districts. Foremost
among these needs was time. Teachers wished they had more time in the
day to meet the needs of individual students, and felt that they did not have
enough time to both cover content and meet students' English development
needs. This problem was compounded by teacher's overall frustration with
the wide variation in ability levels of ELLs in their classrooms, and their
inability to communicate easily or well with parents. They also reported
wanting more time to work collaboratively with colleagues, plan, and learn
from more experienced colleagues. Another reported area of need was for
more help in the classroom from paraprofessionals, and yet another was a
desire for better ELD materials. Teachers in the study had learned about
characteristics of second language learners in professional development, but
overall found that their professional development was not geared purposefully toward helping improve instruction for this population (see also García & Stritikus, 2006).

This finding is echoed in a recent review of professional development
programs about English language learners (Knight & Wiseman, 2006). Despite the large body of knowledge about effective instructional approaches to teaching ELLs, there is a dearth of "guidance for transforming the

effectiveness of in-service teachers" of English language learners via professional development (p. 87). The researchers also found that outside expert-imposed training models, which were common, had mixed impacts on "teacher and student outcomes" (p. 87).[7] Collaborative models of professional development, involving practitioner inquiry and communities of practice, seem to be gaining momentum, but are also, they found, underresearched. This gap signifies a clear need in the field for more research on teacher professional development about teaching ELLs. Teacher educators—who are also, of course, teacher education researchers—are perfectly positioned to conduct such research.

CONTEXTUALIZING TEACHER EDUCATION IN THE AGE OF ACCOUNTABILITY

How should teacher candidates be educated to work within the constraints that assessment pressures create? Newer forms of teacher performance assessments require candidates to engage in formative assessment of their students, but in their jobs as classroom teachers they will be responsible for their students' progress on standardized tests. Marzano (2006) and Popham (2008), among others, discuss ways to use formative assessments in the classroom. But as Ms. Romano's story at the beginning of this chapter showed, it is nearly impossible to avoid assessment pressures at the classroom level.

How should teacher candidates be educated so that they can navigate the rocky shoals of structured curricula in their own classrooms? There is some research on ways teachers finesse (Kersten & Pardo, 2007), augment (Paugh, Carey, King-Jackson, & Russell, 2007), and otherwise argue against these curricula (see Chapter 3). A recent study by Fang, Fu, and Lamme (2004) suggests ways to help current teachers wean themselves away from structured programs—through extensive, teacher-centered professional development. However, it is hard to avoid teaching with structured programs if they are mandated in one's own district. Again, at the classroom level, there is not a lot of scope for pushing back against these curricula—at least not in ways that lead to lasting change.

And, finally, given the pressures to teach to the test, to teach the prepackaged curriculum, and to teach reductive, remedial versions of English, how can we best educate teachers of English language learners—essentially, all future teachers, since that population is growing so fast that teachers will typically have at least *some* ELLs in their mainstream classrooms? Teacher educators across the United States are valiantly addressing these issues, but there is little in the way of answers. At the moment, teachers like Ms. Romano will face increasing pressure if the value-added movement comes to their school districts.

There are specific things teachers can do, or ways teachers can adapt, to try to meet the needs of their English language learners. But individual modifications will never be enough. Even at the district scale, professional development for teachers is not sufficient to halt systemic trends. To do that—to alleviate immediate pressures and reroute our system along a path other than the one we are on—we need massive policy shifts. To begin, we must design and implement measures of accountability, and ways to gauge student progress and teacher effectiveness, other than the methods we currently employ—the focus of my concluding chapter.

CHAPTER 6

Policy and Practice Changes in Assessment and Instruction

My research shows that educational researchers need to reconceive and re-conceptualize the heretofore stand-alone fields of language acquisition, testing and assessment, and literacy studies. It is critical for the functioning of teachers, and the lives of children, that we intertwine our separate knowledge bases. Without looking at these three aspects together, we do not see all that is happening in children's classroom lives, and we will be unable to make comprehensive recommendations for change. In this chapter, I draw together these fields to make some policy and practice recommendations. First, I focus on the teaching and assessment of all children, and then make some more specific recommendations for English language learners. I also address the education of teachers of ELLs and native speakers alike in the age of accountability.

ONE STANDARDIZED, LARGE-SCALE CONTENT-AREA TEST PER EDUCATIONAL LEVEL

The pressure to hold schools accountable runs deep in the United States (Cross, 2010; Vinovskis, 2009), yet constant assessment with high-stakes tools has not led to measurably better performance. Instead, it has led to test-oriented teaching, whose effects we are beginning to know all too well (Ravitch, 2010). Countries whose students score well above U.S. students on literacy and mathematical skills do not mandate testing regimes like ours (Brozo, Shiel, & Topping, 2007; Organisation for Economic Cooperation and Development, 2007). I am not the first to make this point (see, for example, Berliner, 2006; Darling-Hammond, 2010a, 2010b; Forum on Educational Accountability, 2010), and I will probably not be the last. But it bears reiterating here: *Reduced emphasis on high-stakes test results, via a reduc-*

tion of high-stakes testing itself, may be the best way to improve student success and achievement. One immediate, if unlikely, way out of our current overtesting mess is to federally mandate a return to pre-NCLB testing policies. In many states, this means one large-scale content-area standardized test per educational level (one each in elementary, middle, and high school).

This set of once-per-level tests would not necessarily even need to be high-stakes. Data could be used to track progress as it is currently used under NCLB (with some modifications, as I note below), but not to directly penalize children or their teachers as under the current Adequate Yearly Progress model. Eliminating the AYP requirements and sanctions in the revision of the Elementary and Secondary Education Act may be the best step, since the sanctions have not helped the majority of schools bring scores up (Forum on Educational Accountability, 2010). Instead, the use of multiple measures of student achievement can be mandated—not *just* test scores. Diane Ravitch (2010), once a proponent of NCLB, and more recently one of its critics, suggests that schools "use measures of educational accomplishment that are appropriate to the subjects studied, such as research papers in history, essays and stories in literature, research projects in science . . . and other exhibitions of learning" (p. 238). In addition to potentially increasing student achievement levels, the elimination of all but three annual tests in the K-12 years, and the reduction of the stakes of remaining tests, would save money and time, both of which are in short supply in classrooms.

Financial Savings

The money to be saved on testing instruments and scoring could be applied to students' welfare and well-being, to salaries to attract qualified teachers, and/or to materials that enrich classroom learning. One place to look more closely is the testing industry, which has been in flux since the 1994 reauthorization of the Elementary and Secondary Education Act that mandated criterion-referenced, instead of norm-referenced, tests (Toch, 2006). Since each state has its own criteria (i.e., standards), each state must purchase separate, and expensive, tests tied to those criteria. The industry has grown substantially, and lacks any sort of federal oversight. States spend varied amounts of money on their testing programs, according to their budgets and policies, and end up with tests of potentially different quality. As my discussion of events at Laurel Elementary illustrates, programs like Reading First employ their own test makers, who sometimes link tests to existing curricula, creating even more complex testing-as-learning dynamics in the classroom. Toch (2006) recommends that the federal government regulate and provide more oversight in the industry; make more funds available to individual states for test creation to level the playing field between states; and invest in more research and development of new tests. If tied to a general mandate to reduce the number of tests students took, these changes could streamline, and improve, the testing in which schools do engage.

At the moment, although there is increasing activism against what I have described as overtesting practices,[1] it is still difficult for individuals (at the state, district, or school level) to make changes to testing regimes. Take the story of Caitlin McMunn Dooley, a professor of early childhood education at Georgia State University.[2] Starting in 2009, Dooley spent over a year working with her local legislator trying to get a bill through the Georgia State Legislature to eliminate the state's 3-day, 175-minute-per-day test for first- and second-grade students (6-, 7-, and 8-year-olds). The bill stalled—a *long* story—but eventually she got her representative to create a rider on the budget bill to eliminate funding for the early grades test, which would have effectively eliminated the test. When the governor, Sonny Perdue, reviewed the budget bill, he line-item vetoed their rider to the budget bill. Due to the tight state budget, he did not restore funding, but he told the state Department of Education they were not obligated to follow the Assembly's intent and that they could indeed test. It seemed all was lost (Downey, 2010). However, in the end, Georgia's Department of Education, already strapped for cash, did not have the money to run the tests, and the youngest public schoolchildren of Georgia were spared the state test that fiscal year. Money does matter in testing—testing costs a lot, and states sometimes have to do without. A federal mandate for reducing annual testing would help students and save money, and be much more effective in the long term.

Implications of More Time

After financial savings, the most persuasive argument for reducing high-stakes tests of content-area knowledge is that so much *time* might be gained. There would be more time for students to develop and grow at varying rates, and more time for English language learners to acquire academic English skills. If there were less standardized test score data to sift through, there would also be fewer attempts on the part of teachers to try and base instruction on students' often-conflicting test scores. Teachers could then engage in more formative assessments of students' learning and needs. They could use real-time data to differentiate their instruction as needed for their students.

Test-oriented teaching might not disappear with fewer high-stakes tests, but it would be less likely to happen with fewer tests with lower stakes.

Students in the testing grades would have more academic instructional time over the other years, and their teachers might feel less pressure to teach to the test. Testing would no longer necessarily be "how we show what we have learned" in the eyes of students. Students and teachers could show what students have learned in other more meaningful ways—portfolios, performance assessments, real-world projects, to name a few. Our conception of assessment of learning might be broadened away from the high-stakes test score as the only Annual Measurable Achievable Outcome worth looking at, to a series of more meaningful progress measures that teachers, as well as administrators and policy makers, could use to inform instruction.

Yet another trickle-down effect of less testing might just be a reduction in pacing pressures for teachers who are required to use prepackaged curricula. In his discussion of the many things we do not yet understand about teaching English language learners, Goldenberg (2008) argues that at the very least, we know that:

> Effective ELD provides both explicit teaching of *features* of English (such as syntax, grammar, vocabulary, pronunciation, and norms of social usage) and ample, *meaningful* opportunities to *use* English—but we do not know whether there is an optimal balance between the two (much less what it might be). (p. 42, emphasis added)

My data suggest that we often err on the side of too much instruction in the *features* of English, and not enough in the provision of meaningful academic opportunities to *use* English. My data also point to the strict pacing requirements the school district placed on teachers like Ms. Romano as the main culprit for the lack of time for meaningful uses of English. Prepackaged reading curricula are not the culprit, as I have been at pains to show.[3] If school districts wish to continue to use such packages—and they do have many good points—they must reduce the pacing pressures they push down to teachers and students. English language learners and native speakers alike suffer when teachers constantly push them through units in order to stay on track, take the unit test, and get on to the next unit. English language learners in particular do not benefit from fast-tracked curricula. One thing research shows quite clearly is that ELLs need expansive, student-centered curricula with ample time for English language development (de Jong & Harper, 2008; Goldenberg, 2008; Wright, 2010).

Teachers do need to know how to provide opportunities for ELD, and they can learn these skills in credential programs or as practicing teachers in professional development sessions. Many districts, recognizing that relying solely on their prepackaged curricula is not a good strategy, offer training and support for teachers in methods of English language development. It may be tempting to rely on "scientifically proven" approaches to reading instruction because some studies have shown some positives for English language learners (Cheung & Slavin, 2005; Shanahan & Beck, 2006; Slavin et al., 2009). However, it behooves teacher educators and policy makers to ensure that teachers receive in-depth training about how to teach ELLs— across various grades and content areas as needed—so that teachers can use their professional judgment as they teach. A reduction in the number, and stakes, of annual standardized tests would provide more time and money to strengthen practicing teachers' knowledge and thereby contribute directly to the academic growth of all students, English language learners and native speakers alike.

POLICY CHANGES IN THE ASSESSMENT OF ENGLISH LANGUAGE LEARNERS

Many, many changes should be made to our assessment policies. As with my broader suggestions above, the changes would need to be incorporated into the reworking of the Elementary and Secondary Education Act so that states are held accountable for making changes for their English language learners.

Identification of ELLs

My first recommendation has to do with identification of ELLs. A recent paper by Bailey and Kelly (2010) highlights the lack of standardization in the home language surveys most states use as they attempt to meet federal requirements for the identification and placement of ELLs. As they are currently deployed, home language surveys often use ambiguous wording, do not ask enough questions, and ask questions with multiple possible interpretations (e.g., "What was the first language the child learned?" which could be interpreted as their native language, *or* as their dominant language [pp. 9-10]). Concerns over the construct relevance and the accuracy of information lead the researchers to suggest that current home language surveys cause both over- and underidentification of children as English language learners. Recommendations at the federal level pertain to the government's need to help states interpret Title III of NCLB, perhaps through the Office of Civil Rights. At the state level Bailey and Kelly (2010) argue for transparency and the clarification of policies so that schools and districts know what to do and what not to do. They also point out the need for validation studies at the state level to determine if children are being overidentified or missed.

For school-level personnel, ambiguities in the home language survey mean that teachers must attend to the linguistic abilities of their students, and be prepared to help reclassify misidentified children in both directions.

To improve the identification of ELLs, Abedi (2008) proposes an Augmented Classification approach that states might use with their existing data to remove incorrectly labeled ELLs from the ELL pool if needed (to correct faults in existing home language surveys). He suggests using language proficiency scores (on the California English Language Development Tests or similar tests) to deselect children who are not ELLs despite home language survey indicators. Students who reach a proficient achievement level on a standardized English-language test like the CST may also be considered non-ELL, because such high test scores theoretically show that their abilities are on the same level as native speakers who score at or above proficient on such tests. The students left over—those whose scores on the CELDT indicate a lack of complete English proficiency, and those do not score above a cutoff point on the CST—are the ones that the state needs to continue to track.

The classification system Abedi proposes is meant to help districts and states make use of their existing data, but it is not without problems. One problem is the validity of test score cutoffs for different levels (e.g., Below Basic, Basic, Proficient). States have arbitrary cutoff points, and even some native speakers fall below cutoff levels. Few studies have examined the validity of particular cutoff scores (Abedi, 2008; see also Goldenberg & Coleman, 2010). The federal government is providing national cutoff scores as of 2010, and although the validity of their numbers may be untested, at least all states will use the same numbers for their standardized tests, though not for the language tests.

There is one more issue: When parents indicate that their child has a facility in a language other than English on the home language survey, states ought to have access to a language development test in their native language to use to gauge the child's "type and degree of bilingualism" (AERA, APA, & NCME, 1999, p. 95). Ideally, the federal government would make tests in various first languages available so as not to burden states with the creation of primary language tests for potentially small numbers of students. Results on such tests could help states better interpret students' scores on English-language tests, as well as gauge students' overall academic abilities.

Disaggregation of ELL Data

A further policy change for the revision of the ESEA that would help clarify English language learners' progress is to track and disaggregate student data in the ELL subgroup by language proficiency level (Working Group on ELL Policy, 2010). For now, ELL students are lumped together as one, and we have no way to know if individual subgroups are making the same progress, or if there are continuing gaps in language development. Keeping English language learners in the ELL subgroup for accountability purposes only, not for classroom placement, after they are reclassified as proficient would also help researchers and policy makers understand the full progress ELLs make as they continue through the grades. At the moment, our ELL subgroup numbers are somewhat depressed because proficient speakers leave the subgroup, artificially lowering the group's scores and blurring the overall picture of student progress in English after reclassification.

Hakuta, Butler, and Witt (2000) recommend that the entire elementary period be considered as one of English Language Development, since students typically take 5 to 7 years to reach academic English fluency. Tracking by English language learner subgroup would help states and districts discover if their reclassification patterns are within, or outside of, these 5 to 7 years. These kinds of data are needed in order to hold states accountable for the progress their ELLs are or are not making. Finally, while readjusting data tracking in the subgroups, statistics on ELL representation in special education programs need to be analyzed by ELL subgroup. Such analyses would shed light on placement patterns at multiple levels and indicate where ELLs may be overrepresented (Artiles, Rueda, Salazar, & Higareda, 2005).

Appropriateness of Tests for ELLs

As the scores of English language learners are tracked by subgroup, states should be required to make sure that the English-language standardized tests they use are designed for ELLs. They should be "proven to provide inferences of comparable reliability and validity for ELL and non-ELL students" (Working Group on ELL Policy, 2010, p. 5). As the AERA, APA, & NCME (1999) standards note, "when a test is intended for use with test takers who differ linguistically from those for whom the test was designed, establishing equivalence poses a greater challenge" (p. 93). It is not an impossible challenge, but one that needs to be thoughtfully, and seriously, addressed. The equivalence argument should be extended to at least three English language learner levels as specified by NCLB/ESEA (beginning, intermediate, and advanced), and test makers, or test purchasers, should be required to establish the equivalence of their constructs for each group. With this step, whether the nation goes forward to testing less often or continues with the annual testing mania, at least the data used to interpret the progress of ELLs in the content areas will be reliable.

Test Accommodations for ELLs

One last area worth noting here is the various kinds of accommodations test administrators can make for English language learners taking high-stakes tests. These might include providing dictionaries in students' first languages, giving more time, and allowing for translation of directions. However, not all accommodations have been shown to work to reduce test bias against ELLs, or to increase the validity of standardized tests for ELL populations (cf. Haladyna, 2002). One avenue of approach in the meantime—while test makers work on reliability and validity concerns—is to make accommodations for English language learners that *have* been proven to reduce construct-irrelevant errors, yet maintain test integrity. For example, "linguistic modification of content-based test items" (Abedi & Gándara, 2006, p. 41) can ensure that test questions do not use overly complex language that obscures the point of the test item for ELLs.

Another temporary solution is for states to set content-area performance standards for students at each level of English proficiency, which California has done with its English Language Development standards for the English Language Arts (CDE, 2002). The California ELD standards are organized by age and English ability. The standards group children in 3-year increments (kindergarten–second grade, third–fifth, sixth–eighth, and ninth–twelfth grades) and simultaneously by English language proficiency level within those groups (from beginning to advanced, as measured by the California English Language Development Test). Thus, a third-grade teacher can look at the Grade 3-5 standards to see what each of his or her English language learners should be able to do, depending on their CELDT level, to get close to meeting different language arts standards. At the least, these ELD standards help teachers know what constitutes developmentally appropriate responses from students to their lesson plans.

POLICY AND CONTENT CHANGES FOR TEACHER EDUCATION REGARDING ENGLISH LANGUAGE LEARNERS

Teacher education programs are convenient targets for blame; they are also frequently sites of problem-solving. For instance, when the California State University's exit survey of Teacher Credential Candidates data showed that graduates felt underprepared to work with English language learners, the system Chancellor placed credential programs under an extensive "Improvement and Accountability Plan." Each campus had to create detailed plans for their own program's improvement and document the changes to the Chancellor's satisfaction. Since credential program content in California (and many other states) is strictly delineated by the state's Department of Education and the Commission on Teacher Credentialing, when faculty planned changes in response the IAP, they had to do so within the tight confines of a predetermined set of course offerings and a controlled number of course units. Whether all of this activity—analysis, planning, documenting change—will lead to better scores for ELLs is debatable. I have used the example to show one of the many ways teacher credential programs act as magnets for criticism, and yet are seen as spaces with potential solutions.

Program Changes

Faculty of teacher education programs are most often the researchers uncovering the gaps in their own programs, by following their graduates, or conducting national and international research on teacher learning and student success. These are the people who can best explain how, and where, to make ELL-related changes in their programs. Depending on a program's current offerings and structure, there are a number of kinds of changes discussed in current research on teacher preparation. One necessary change is to make English language learners visible in teacher education program content and teacher candidate assessment across the board. De Jong and Harper (2008) found that ELLs are often "invisible in education documents, particularly with regard to the linguistic diversity they add to the classroom" (p. 130). An unfortunate result of the exclusion of ELLs from program content over time has been the development of separate sets of standards and waivers for ELLs. A second change on which many researchers agree is to make 1-year intensive clinical placements for teacher candidates mandatory, and to embed performance assessments in that year-long experience (Darling-Hammond, 2006, 2010a; Hammerness, Darling-Hammond, Grossman, Rust, & Shulman, 2005). Extensive, intensive clinical preparation for candidates would ensure that they have ample time to practice what they learn in credential program classes—about English language learners, for example—in real contexts with the support of qualified mentor teachers.

Enhancing Teacher Knowledge

In addition to these two areas of program change, there are two main bodies of knowledge that many researchers agree should be enhanced in teacher education programs: *processes of second language acquisition* and *methods of informal assessment to inform teaching and assess learning*. Snow and Fillmore's (2000) discussion, *What Teachers Need to Know*

About Language is well known in teacher education circles, but in my experience, its content does not penetrate far enough into the knowledge bases of teacher candidates. Nor do accompanying strategies for how to scaffold and promote academic discourse in English for English language learners (Gersten, 1999). Indeed, results from de Jong and Harper's (2008) research on an "ESL-infused teacher preparation program" (p. 139) showed that it was easier for teacher educators to incorporate cultural rather than linguistic issues in their courses. This finding, they argue, parallels the dearth of research on linguistic diversity in the literature on multiculturalism in contrast to the topics of ethnicity, gender, socioeconomic status, and special needs. Echoing Gersten (1999), they found that teachers of ELLs particularly needed practice "providing sustained and extended opportunities for social and academic language development" (p. 141).

Teacher knowledge of methods of assessment to inform instruction and assess students' learning is also critical for the success of English language learners. If teacher candidates have a sound grounding in processes of second language acquisition, they can apply that knowledge to informal assessments of their students. They will not need to wait for the results of statewide language development tests, or rely on old tests, but can use timely data they gather to help them decide what their students still need to know. This kind of learning would work best in teacher education programs that offer coursework alongside of, or in close conjunction to, clinical settings, so that candidates can practice what they are learning under the guidance of more experienced mentor teachers. Given the increasing number of language learners in America, teacher educations programs need to do more. Some recommend tacking on additional courses in second language acquisition to sets of coursework (Lucas, Villegas, & Freedson-Gonzalez, 2008), while others suggest infusing this knowledge into entire programs (Gándara & Maxwell-Jolly, 2006; Téllez & Waxman, 2006b).

IN CLOSING: LEARNING IN THE AGE OF ACCOUNTABILITY

If this book has shown nothing else, it is my hope that readers have more of a sense of what it is like to be an English language learner during the accountability turn, in a school setting where teachers are not trusted, where children are overtested, and where, if students cannot answer multiple-choice questions about a book correctly, they are not considered good readers. Those of us invested in the American education system need to reform its worst tendencies toward overassessment, especially given the changing composition and dynamics of American classrooms. These needed reforms may occur in the realm of research, where, as I have noted, we need to know so much more than we currently do about how to best assess progress in English language development, how to best teach English language learners, and how to help teachers in this process. They may also occur in the realm of practice, where we need fewer tests, and where teachers need more time and space to teach.

Though we as a nation are becoming ever more diverse—and more fractured—linguistically, culturally, and socioeconomically, our public schools remain sites of possibility, unity, and growth (cf. Genishi & Dyson, 2009). We need to find alternative ways to help our students develop the intelligence they bring to school. We need to help them become ethical, thoughtful members of our society. At the moment, we are trapped in the first step of this process: assessment. The intense pressures brought on by our national passion for accountability need to be acknowledged, but also appropriately contextualized. Right now, the burdens fall mostly on the shoulders of individual teachers such as Ms. Romano. The burdens should lie with all of us, and it is up to all of us to lighten them.

Notes

Chapter 1

1. For positive interpretations of Reading First's results, see Bean, Draper, Turner, & Zigmond (2010), Beck (2010), Carlisle, Cortina, & Zeng (2010), Dole, Hosp, Nelson, & Hosp (2010), and Foorman, Petscher, Lefsky, & Toste (2010). These articles appeared in the same themed issue of the *Journal of Literacy Research* in 2010.

2. See Wiley & Wright (2004), Wright (2005), and Gándara, Losen, August, Uriarte, Gomez, & Hopkins (2010) for in-depth discussions of anti-immigration movements in Arizona, California, and Massachusetts.

3. See Stritikus (2002) and Wright (2002) for accounts of classroom life post-Proposition 227.

4. See, for example, Bomer, Dworin, May, & Semingson (2008), Flores, Cousin, & Díaz (1991), Gay (2000), Gonzáles, Moll, & Amanti (2005), and Haberman (1996).

5. See, for example, Altwerger (2005), Arya, Laster, & Jin (2005), Valli et al. (2008), Valli & Chambliss (2007), and Wiltz & Wilson (2006).

Chapter 2

1. See Abedi (2007, 2008), August & Shanahan (2006a, 2007), García, McKoon, & August (2006a, 2006b), Goldenberg (2008), and Goldenberg & Coleman (2010) for what we do know.

2. For more discussion about the costs of assessment, see Wright (2006) and Zellmer, Frontier, & Pheifer (2006).

3. For some documentation of these effects, see Hoffman et al. (2003), Menken (2008), Paris, Lawton, Turner, & Roth, (1991), Perlstein (2007), Valli et al. (2008), and Wright (2002).

4. Dooley & Assaf (2009), Valli et al. (2008), and Zellmer, Frontier, & Phiefer (2006) discuss similar consequences.

Chapter 3

1. This discussion skirts a larger issue of the quest for science in education, which is beyond the scope of my point here. See Labaree (2006) and Lagemann (2000), as well as Zimmerman (2010).

2. See Foorman, Francis, Fletcher, Schatschneider, & Mehta (1998) for a classic example of this reasoning.

3. P. David Pearson and Richard Allington do manage to enter this fray on a regular basis. See Allington (2001, 2002, 2009), Pearson (2004, 2010), and Pearson & Hiebert (2010).

4. For discussions of these elisions and their ramifications, see Allington (2002), Cummins (2007), Garan (2002, 2004), Krashen (2002), and Yatvin (2002).

5. For *opposing* perspectives on teaching the parts before the whole, see Dyson (2006) and Genishi & Dyson (2009). On teaching fluency before comprehension, see Allington (2009), Applegate, Applegate, & Modla (2009), Krashen (2002), and Samuels (2007); and on privileging one standardized textual interpretation over others see Aukerman (2007, 2008).

6. See note 5.

7. This list is long, but by no means comprehensive: Arya, Laster, & Jin (2005), Ávila, Zacher Pandya, Griffo, & Pearson (forthcoming, October 2011), Jaeger (2006), Lee, Ajayi, & Richards (2007), Samway & Pease-Alvarez (2005), Shelton (2005), and Valli & Buese (2007).

8. See Nichols (2006) for similar conclusions about an Australian "thinking technology."

9. Boyd and Rubin (2002) have investigated the ways teacher questioning—when it is contingent on student responses—can elicit and foster discussion by English language learners.

Chapter 4

1. For a discussion of this label itself, see Gutiérrez & Orellana (2006) and Orellana & Gutiérrez (2006).

2. De Jong & Harper (2008), Lee (1994), and Olsen (1997, 2000) refer to the desire of some language learners to fade quietly into the background to divert attention away from themselves.

3. For documentation of a similar phenomenon, see Weinstein (2002).

4. Teresa's family home was similar in many ways to the home of Alessandro, the English language learner whose difficult trajectory through parochial schools in Chicago is described by Chris Carger (1996).

5. Zlolniski (2006) provides one accounting of the pressures of being undocumented in the workplace.

6. Stories abound about children whose parents have gone home to care for a relative, only to be unable to return and reunite with their child/ren (Hondagneu-Sotelo, 2006; Hondagneu-Sotelo & Ávila, 1997; Nazario, 2007).

7. See Bailey & Kelly's (2010) discussion of the variability and fallibility of home language surveys across the United States. Also see Abedi (2008) for definitions and discussions about the HLS.

8. There are many more recommended strategies for developing English language learners' writing skills. See, for example, the work of De Jong & Harper (2008), Echeverria, Vogt, & Short (2008), Genesee, Lindholm-Leary, Saunders, & Christian (2005, 2006), Goldenberg & Coleman (2010), Hudelson (1994), and Xu (2010), to list a very few.

9. See, for example, Gándara & Contreras (2009), Gándara, Losen, August, Uriarte, Gómez, & Hopkins (2010), Garcia & Cuéllar (2006), Reese (2002), Suárez-Orozco & Todorova (2003), Suárez-Orozco, Suárez-Orozco, & Todorova (2008), Valdès (2001), and Valenzuela (1999).

10. In December 2010, the U.S. Senate blocked a bill supported by President Obama that would have created citizenship pathways for undocumented youth who serve in the military for at least 2 years, or who complete at least 2 years of college. Writers of the 2010 DREAM Act (Development, Relief, and Education for Alien Minors) argue that it is in the country's best interests to educate all students to their best potential, and note that undocumented students face huge financial barriers to college without the law's eventual passage (Suárez-Orozco & Suárez-Orozco, 2009). Supporters have pledged to continue to try and pass the DREAM Act in 2011 in the new Republican-controlled Congress.

11. Berliner (2006); Campbell, Ramey, Pungello, Sparling, & Miller-Johnson (2002); Duncan, Yeung, Brooks-Gunn, & Smith (1998).

12. Capps et al. (2002); Capps et al. (2005); Carger (1996); Gándara & Contreras (2009).

Chapter 5

1. For more examples of clashes between teacher beliefs about ELLs' needs and prepackaged curricula, see Pease-Alvarez & Samway (2008), Ruiz & Morales-Ellis (2005), and Samway & Pease-Alvarez (2005).

2. The state of Connecticut was one of the first to pilot teacher performance assessments, based on the work of researchers in the Teacher Assessment Project at Stanford University (Pecheone & Stansbury, 1996; Pecheone & Chung, 2006).

3. Pecheone & Chung (2006) also write about the costs associated with developing and implementing the PACT assessment system, noting especially the high cost of creating the assessment itself as well as the costs associated with faculty reassignments in order to place PACT assessments in existing courses and to compensate teaching supervisors and mentors for scoring the assessment.

4. In late September 2010, Robert Ruelas, one of the teachers whose scores had been publicized in the *Los Angeles Times* report, committed suicide (Zavis & Barboza, 2010). According to news reports, Ruelas did not leave a note, but his colleagues said he had been upset about his overall rating as "less effective" compared to his coworkers.

5. For a more detailed discussion of the statistical pitfalls inherent in value-added measurement, see Baker et al. (2010).

6. I have argued elsewhere (Zacher Pandya, forthcoming, 2012b) that a scale approach—one that accounts for events and actions at different scales, from the classroom to the nation—helps explain why efforts at reform are more difficult than they might first seem.

7. Ávila, Zacher Pandya, Griffo, & Pearson (2011) discuss similar results from their professional development project in reading, conducted in the midst of a state takeover of the school district complete with a top-down language arts curriculum mandate.

Chapter 6

1. See, for example, the Fairtest group (www.fairtest.org); Susan Ohanian's website (http://www.susanohanian.org); and Kozol (2007).

2. Many thanks to Caitlin McMunn Dooley for commenting on my rendition of her testing-protesting story. Errors in relaying her story here are all mine.

3. Costigan (2008) and Cuban (2009) both provide examples of successful teachers in high-stakes settings who use mandated curricula.

References

Abedi, J. (Ed.) (2007). *English language proficiency assessment in the nation: Current status and future practice.* Davis: University of California.

Abedi, J. (2008). Classification system for English language learners: Issues and recommendations. *Educational Measurement: Issues and Practice, 27*(3), 17–31.

Abedi, J., & Gándara, P. (2006). Performance of English language learners as a subgroup in large-scale assessment: Interaction of research and policy. *Educational Measurement: Issues and Practice, 25*(4), 36–46.

Agee, J. (2004). Negotiating a teaching identity: An African American teacher's struggle to teach in test-driven contexts. *Teachers College Record, 106*(4), 747–774.

Albers, P., & Harste, J. C. (2007). The arts, new literacies, and multimodality. *English Education, 40*(1), 6–20.

Allington, R. L. (2001). *What really matters for struggling readers: Designing research-based programs.* New York: Longman.

Allington, R. L. (2002). *Big brother and the national reading curriculum: How ideology trumped evidence.* Portsmouth, NH: Heinemann.

Allington, R. L. (2009). *What really matters in fluency: Research-based practices across the curriculum.* Boston: Allyn & Bacon.

Altwerger, B. (Ed.). (2005). *Reading for profit: How the bottom line leaves kids behind.* Portsmouth, NH: Heinemann.

Alvarez, L., & Corn, J. (2007). Exchanging assessment for accountability: The implications of high-stakes reading assessment for English learners. *Language Arts, 85*(5), 354–365.

American Educational Research Association, American Psychological Association, & National Council on Measurement in Education. (1999). *Standards for educational and psychological testing 1999.* Washington, DC: American Educational Research Association Publications.

Applegate, V., Applegate, A. V., & Modla, V. (2009). "She's my best reader; she just can't comprehend": Studying the relationship between fluency and comprehension. *The Reading Teacher, 62*(6), 512–521.

Artiles, A., Klingner, J., Sullivan, A., & Fierros, E. (2010). Shifting landscapes of professional practices: English learner special education placement in English-only states. In P. Gándara & M. Hopkins (Eds.), *Forbidden language: English learners and restrictive language policies* (pp. 102–117). New York: Teachers College Press.

Artiles, A., Rueda, R., Salazar, J., & Higareda, I. (2005). Within-group diversity in minority disproportionate representation: English language learners in urban school districts. Exceptional Children, 71(3), 283–300.

Arya, P., Laster, B., & Jin, L. (2005). An open look at the Open Court program. In B. Altwerger (Ed.), *Reading for profit: How the bottom line leaves kids behind* (pp. 128–141). Portsmouth, NH: Heinemann.

Assaf, L. (2005). One reading specialist's response to high-stakes testing pressures. *The Reading Teacher, 60*(2), 158–167.

Assembly Bill 540 (2001, October 13). California State Assembly (Firebaugh & Maldonado). Retrieved from: http://leginfo.ca.gov/pub/01–02/bill/asm/ab_0501–0550/ab_540_bill_20011013_history.html

Atwell, N. (1998). *In the middle: New understandings about writing, reading, and learning* (2nd ed.). Portsmouth, NH: Boynton/Cook.

August, D., & Shanahan, T. (Eds.). (2006a). *Developing literacy in second-language learners: Report of the National Literacy Panel on language-minority children and youth*. Mahwah, NJ: Erlbaum.

August, D., & Shanahan, T. (2006b). Synthesis: Instruction and professional development. In D. August & T. Shanahan (Eds.), *Developing literacy in second-language learners: Report of the National Literacy Panel on language-minority children and youth* (pp. 351–363). Mahwah, NJ: Erlbaum.

August, D., & Shanahan, T. (Eds.). (2007). *Developing reading and writing in second-language learners: Lessons from the report of the national literacy panel on language-minority children and youth*. New York: Routledge.

Aukerman, M. (2006, October). Who's afraid of the big "bad" answer? *Educational Leadership, 64*(2), 36–41.

Aukerman, M. (2007). When reading it wrong is getting it right: Shared evaluation pedagogy among struggling fifth grade readers. *Research in the Teaching of English, 42*(1), 56–103.

Aukerman, M. (2008). In praise of wiggle room: Locating comprehension in unlikely places. *Language Arts, 86*(1), 52–60.

Ávila, J., Underwood, C., & Woodbridge, S. (2008). "I'm the expert now": Digital storytelling and transforming literacies among displaced children. In D. McInerney & A.D. Liem (Eds.), *Research on sociocultural influences on motivation and learning: Teaching and learning: International best practice* (Vol. 8, pp. 349–376). Charlotte, NC: Information Age Publishing.

Ávila, J., & Zacher Pandya, J. (forthcoming, 2012). The future of critical literacies in U.S. schools: An introduction. *Theory into Practice*.

Ávila, J., Zacher Pandya, J., Griffo, V., & Pearson, P. D. (2011). Conducting instructional intervention research in the midst of a state takeover. *Pedagogies: An International Journal, 6*(4), 30–45. doi: 10.1080/1554480X.2011.532085

Bailey, A., & Kelly, K. (2010). The use and validity of home language surveys in state English language proficiency assessment systems: A review and issues perspective. *The EVEA Project*. Retrieved from http://www.eveaproject.com/doc/HLS White Paper 2010.pdf

Baker, K. (1999). *Basics of structured English immersion for language minority students*. Washington, DC: Center for Equal Opportunity.

Baker, E., Barton, P., Darling-Hammond, L., Haertel, E., Ladd, H., Linn, R., Ravitch, D., Rothstein, R., Shavelson, R., & Shepard, L. (2010). *Problems with the use of student test scores to evaluate teachers.* Washington, DC: Economic Policy Institute.

Bandeira de Mello, V., Blankenship, C., & McLaughlin, D. H. (2009). *Mapping state proficiency standards onto NAEP scales: 2005–2007* (NCES 2010–456). Washington, DC: National Center for Education Statistics, Institute of Education Sciences, U.S. Department of Education.

Bandura, A. (2002). Social cognitive theory in cultural context. *Applied Psychology: An International Review, 51*(2), 269–290.

Bean, R., Draper, J., Turner, G., & Zigmond, N. (2010). Reading first in Pennsylvania: Achievement findings after five years. *Journal of Literacy Research, 42*(1), 5–26.

Beck, I. (2010). Half-full or half-empty. *Journal of Literacy Research, 42*(1), 94–99.

Berliner, D. (2006). Our impoverished view of educational research. *Teachers College Record, 108*(6), 949–995.

Black, P., Harrison, C., Lee, C., Marshall, B., & William, W. (2004). *The nature and value of formative assessment for learning.* Retrieved from www.kcl.ac.uk/content/1/c4/73/57/formative.pdf

Black, P., & William, D. (1998). Inside the black box: Raising standards through classroom assessment. *Phi Delta Kappan 80*(2), 139–144, 146–148. Retrieved from http://www.pdkintl.org/kappan/kbla9810.htm

Black, R. (2008). *Adolescents and online fan fiction.* New York: Peter Lang.

Blank, M., Jacobson, R., & Pearson, S. (2009, Summer). A coordinated effort: Well-conducted partnerships meet students' academic, health, and social service needs. *American Educator, 30*–36.

Bomer, R., Dworin, J., May, L., & Semingson, P. (2008). Miseducating teachers about the poor: A critical analysis of Ruby Payne's claims about poverty. *Teachers College Record, 10*(11). Retrieved from http://www.tcrecord.org/content.asp?ContentsId=14591

Borman, G. D., Dowling, N. M., & Schneck, C. (2007). *The national randomized field trial of Open Court Reading.* Madison, WI: University of Wisconsin Press.

Borman, G. D., Slavin, R., Cheung, A., Chamberlain, A., Madden, N. A., & Chambers, B. (2007). Final reading outcomes of the national randomized field trial of Success for All. *American Educational Research Journal, 44*(3), 701–731.

Boyd, M. & Rubin, D. (2002). Elaborated student talk in an elementary ESoL classroom. *Research in the Teaching of English, 32*(4), 495–530.

Bracey, G.W. (2008). Cut scores, NAEP achievement levels and their discontents. *School Administrator, 65*(6), 20–23.

Brill, M. T. (2005). Food from the 'hood: A garden of hope. In SRA/McGraw-Hill (Ed.), *Open court reading: 4th grade.* Columbus, OH: McGraw-Hill.

Brozo, W., Shiel, G., & Topping, K. (2007). Engagement in reading: Lessons learned from three PISA countries. *Journal of Adolescent & Adult Literacy, 51*(4), 304–315.

Buddin, R. (2010). How effective are Los Angeles elementary teachers and schools? *The Los Angeles Times.* Retrieved from http://www.latimes.com/media/acrobat/2010–08/55538493.pdf

Buddin, R., McCaffrey, D., Kirby, S., & Xia, N. (2007). *Merit pay for Florida teachers: Design and implementation issues* (Working paper). Santa Monica, CA: Rand.

Bunch, G. C., Aguirre, J., & Téllez, K. (2009). Beyond the scores: Using candidate responses on high stakes performance assessment to inform teacher preparation for English learners. *Issues in Teacher Education, 18*(1), 103–128.

California Commission on Teacher Credentialing. (2001). *California teaching performance expectations.* Retrieved from http://www.ctc.ca.gov/educator-prep/TPA-California.html

California Department of Education. (2002). *English-language development standards for California public schools, kindergarten through grade twelve.* Sacramento: Author.

California Department of Education. (2006). *Public school summary statistics.* Retrieved from http://www.cde.ca.gov/ds/sd/cb/sums05.asp

California Department of Education. (2007). *California standardized testing and reporting (STAR) program.* Retrieved from http://star.cde.ca.gov/star2007/

California Department of Education. (2008). *CST in writing parent guide.* Retrieved from http://cde.ca.gov/ta/tg/sr/documents/guidecstwrit08.doc

Camarota, S. (2005). *Immigrants at mid-decade: A snapshot of America's foreign-born population in 2005.* Retrieved from Center for Immigration Studies website: http://www.cis.org/articles/2005/back1405.html

Campano, G. (2007). *Immigrant students and literacy: Reading, writing, and remembering.* New York: Teachers College Press.

Campbell, F. A., Ramey, C. T., Pungello, E., Sparling, J., & Miller-Johnson, S. (2002). Early childhood education: Young adult outcomes from the abecedarian project. *Applied Developmental Science, 6*(1), 42–57.

Capps, R., Fix, M., Murray, J., Ost, J., Passel, J., & Hernandez, S. H. (2005). *The new demography of America's schools: Immigration and the No Child Left Behind act.* Washington, DC: The Urban Institute.

Capps, R., Ku, L., Fix, M., Furgiuele, C., Passel, J., Ramchand, R., McNiven, S., & Perez-Lopez, D. (2002). *How are immigrants faring after welfare reform? Preliminary evidence from Los Angeles and New York City—Final report.* Washington, DC: The Urban Institute.

Carger, C. L. (1996). *Of borders and dreams: A Mexican-American experience of urban education.* New York: Teachers College Press.

Carlisle, J., Cortina, K., & Zeng, J. (2010). Reading achievement in reading first schools in Michigan. *Journal of Literacy Research, 42*(1), 49–70.

Cazden, C., & Mehan, H. (1989). Principles for sociology and anthropology: Context, code, classroom, and culture. In C. Cazden & H. Mehan (Eds.), *Knowledge base for the beginning teacher* (pp. 47–57). New York: Pergamon.

Chavez, L. (1991). *Shadowed lives: Undocumented immigrants in American society.* New York: Harcourt Brace Jovanovich College Publishers.

Cheung, A., & Slavin, R. (2005). Effective reading programs for English language learners and other language minority students. *Bilingual Research Journal, 29*(2), 241–267.

Chung, R. R. (2008). Beyond assessment: Performance assessments in teacher education. *Teacher Education Quarterly, 35*(1), 7–28.

Conner, J. M., Greene, B. G., & Munroe, K. (2004). *An experimental study of the instructional effectiveness of the Harcourt Reading Program in academically at-risk schools in the Philadelphia city school district.* Bloomington, IN: Educational Research, Institute of America.

Costigan, A. (2008). *Teaching authentic language arts in a test-driven era.* New York: Routledge.

Crawford, J. (2004). *Educating English learners.* Bilingual Education Services, Los Angeles, CA.

Cross, C. T. (2010). *Political education national policy comes of age* (updated ed.). New York: Teachers College Press.

Cuban, L. (2009). *Hugging the middle: How teachers teach in an era of testing and accountability.* New York: Teachers College Press.

Cummins, J. (1981). Age on arrival and immigrant second language learning in Canada: A reassessment. *Applied Linguistics, 11*(2), 132–149.

Cummins, J. (2000). *Language, power and pedagogy: Bilingual children in the crossfire.* Clevedon, UK: Multilingual Matters.

Cummins, J. (2007). Pedagogies for the poor? Realigning reading instruction for low-income students with scientifically based research. *Educational Researcher, 36*(9), 564–572.

Damon, W. (1995). Dispositions and teacher assessment: The need for a more rigorous definition. *Journal of Teacher Education, 58*(5), 365–369.

Darling-Hammond, L. (2006). *Powerful teacher education: Lessons from exemplary programs.* San Francisco: Jossey-Bass.

Darling-Hammond, L. (2010a). Teacher education and the American future. *Journal of Teacher Education, 61*(1–2), 35–47.

Darling-Hammond, L. (2010b). *Performance counts: Assessment systems that support high-quality learning.* Washington, DC: Council of Chief State School Officers.

Darling-Hammond, L., & Bransford, J. (Eds.). (2005). *Preparing teachers for a changing world: What teachers should learn and be able to do.* San Francisco, CA: Jossey-Bass.

Darling-Hammond, L., & Falk, B. (1999). Using standards and assessments to support student learning. *Phi Delta Kappan, 73*(3), 190–199.

De Jong, E., & Harper, C. (2008). ESL is good teaching "plus": Preparing standard curriculum teachers for all learners. In M. Brisk (Ed.), *Language, culture, and community in teacher education* (pp. 127–148). New York: Routledge for the American Association of Colleges for Teacher Education.

Delgado-Gaitan, C. (1987). Traditions and transitions in the learning process of Mexican children: An ethnographic view. In G. Spindler & L. Spindler (Eds.), *Interpretive ethnography of education at home and abroad* (pp. 333–359). Mahwah, NJ: Erlbaum.

Diaz-Rico, L., & Weed, K. (2006). *The crosscultural, language, and academic development handbook: A complete K–12 reference guide* (3rd ed.). Boston, MA: Pearson.

Dillon, S. (2009, October 29). Federal researchers find lower standards in schools. *The New York Times.* Retrieved from http://www.nytimes.com/2009/10/30/education/30educ.html?scp=19&sq=texas+score+test&st=nyt

Dillon, S. (2010, December 3). Teacher ratings get a new look, pushed by a rich watcher. *The New York Times.* Retrieved from http://www.nytimes.com/2010/12/04/education/04teacher.html

District of Columbia Public Schools. (2010). *IMPACT: District of Columbia public schools effectiveness assessment system for school based personnel, 2010–2011.* Washington, DC: Author.

Dole, J., Hosp, J., Nelson, K., & Hosp, M. (2010). Second opinions on the reading first initiative: The view from Utah. *Journal of Literacy Research, 42*(1), 27–48.

Dole, J., & Osborn, J. (2003). Elementary language arts textbooks: A decade of change. In J. Flood, D. Lapp, J. Squire, & J. Jensen (Eds.), *Handbook on research on the teaching the English language arts* (2nd ed.; pp. 631–639). Mahwah, NJ: Erlbaum.

Dooley, C. M. (2006). One teacher's resistance to the pressures of test mentality. *Language Arts, 82*(3), 177–185.

Dooley, C. M., & Assaf, L. (2009). Contexts matter: Two teachers' language arts instruction in this high-stakes era. *Journal of Literacy Research, 41*(3), 354–91.

Downey, M. (2010, March 30). Bill to dump CRCT in early grades goes nowhere. Why? *Atlanta Journal-Constitution.* Retrieved from http://blogs.ajc.com/get-schooled-blog/2010/03/30/bill-to-dump-crct-in-early-grades-goes-nowhere-why/

Dubin, J. (2009, Summer). These kids are alright. *American Educator,* 8–15.

Duncan, A. (2009). *Robust data gives us the roadmap to reform.* Addresses to the Fourth Annual IES Research Conference. August, 2009. Retrieved from http://www2.ed.gov/news/speeches/2009/06/06082009.html

Duncan, G., Yeung, J. W., Brooks-Gunn, J., & Smith, J. R. (1998). How much does childhood poverty affect the life chances of children? *American Sociological Review, 63*(3), 406–423.

Dúran, R. P. (2008). Assessing English-language learners' achievement. *Review of Research in Education, 32*(1), 292–327. doi: 10.3102/0091732X07309372

Durkin, D. (1978–79). What classroom observations reveal about reading comprehension instruction. *Reading Research Quarterly, 14*(4), 481–533.

Dutro, E. (2010). What 'Hard times' means: Mandated curricula, class-privileged assumptions, and the lives of poor children. *Research in the Teaching of English, 44*(3), 255–291.

Dworin, J., & Bomer, R. (2008). What we all (supposedly) know about the poor: A critical discourse analysis of Ruby Payne's "Framework." *English Education, 42*(2), 101–121.

Dyson, A. H. (1997). *Writing superheroes: Contemporary childhood, popular culture, and classroom literacy.* New York and London: Teachers College Press.

Dyson, A. H. (1999). Transforming transfer: Unruly children, contrary texts, and the persistence of the pedagogical order. *Review of Research in Education, 24,* 141–171.

Dyson, A. H. (2006). On saying it right (write): "Fix-its" in the foundations of learning to write. *Research in the Teaching of English, 41*(1), 8–42.

Echevarria, J., & Graves, A. (2003). *Sheltered content instruction: Teaching English-language learners with diverse abilities* (2nd ed.). Boston: AB Longman.

Echeverria, J., Vogt, M. E., & Short, D. (2008). *Making content comprehensible for English learners: The SIOP model* (3rd ed.). Boston, MA: Pearson.

Education Data Partnership. (2009). *Understanding California's standardized testing and reporting (STAR) program.* Retrieved from http://www.ed-data.k12.ca.us/Articles/Article.asp?title=Understanding the STAR

Ellis, R. (2008). *Principles of instructed second language acquisition.* Retrieved from Center for Applied Linguistics website: http://www.cal.org

Fang, Z., Fu, D., & Lamme, L. L. (2004). From scripted instruction to teacher empowerment: Supporting literacy teachers to make pedagogical transitions. *Literacy, 38*(1), 58–64.

Felch, J., Song, J., & Smith, D. (2010, August 14). Who's teaching L.A.'s kids? *The Los Angeles Times.* Retrieved from http://www.latimes.com/news/local/la-me-teachers-value-20100815,0,258862,full.story

Fillmore, L.W. (2000). Loss of family languages: Should educators be concerned? *Theory into Practice, 39*(4), 203–210.

Flores, B., Cousin, P. T., & Diaz, E. (1991). Transforming deficit myths about learning, language, and culture. *Language Arts, 68*(5), 369–379.

Foorman, B. R., Francis, D. J., Fletcher, J. M., Schatschneider, C., & Mehta, P. (1998). The role of instruction in learning to read: Preventing reading failure in at-risk children. *Journal of Educational Psychology, 90*(1), 37–55.

Foorman, B. R., Petscher, Y., Lefsky, E., & Toste, J. (2010). Reading first in Florida: Five years of improvement. *Journal of Literacy Research, 42*(1), 71–93.

Forum on Educational Accountability (FEA). (2010). *FEA recommendations for improving ESEA/NCLB—summary.* Retrieved from http://edaccountability.org

Freire, P. (1970/2000). *Pedagogy of the oppressed* (30th Anniversary Edition, with introduction by Donaldo Macedo [Ed.]). New York: Continuum.

Frey, N., & Hiebert, E. (2003). Teacher-based assessment of literacy learning. In J. Flood, D. Lapp, J. Squire, & J. Jensen (Eds.), *Handbook of research on teaching the English language arts* (pp. 608–618). Mahwah, NJ: Erlbaum.

Fry, R. (2003). *Hispanic youth dropping out of U.S. schools: Measuring the challenge.* Washington, DC: Pew Hispanic Center.

Fusarelli, L. (2004). The potential impact of the No Child Left Behind act on equity and diversity in American education. *Educational Policy, 18*(1), 71–94.

Gabriel, T. (2010, June 10). Cheat sheet: Under pressure, teachers tamper with tests. *The New York Times.* Retrieved from http://www.nytimes.com/2010/06/11/education/11cheat.html

Gamse, B. C., Bloom, H. S., Kemple, J., & Jacob, R. T. (2008). *Reading First impact study: Interim report* (NCEE 2008–4016). Washington, DC: National Center for Education Evaluation and Regional Assistance, Institute of Education Sciences, U.S. Department of Education.

Gamse, B.C., Jacob, R.T., Horst, M., Boulay, B., & Unlu, F. (2008). *Reading First impact study final report* (NCEE 2009–4038). Washington, DC: National Center for Education Evaluation and Regional Assistance, Institute of Education Sciences, U.S. Department of Education.

Gándara, P., & Contreras, F. (2009). *The Latino education crisis: The consequences of failed social policies.* Cambridge, MA: Harvard University Press.

Gándara, P., Losen, D., August, D., Uriarte, M., Gomez, M. C., & Hopkins, M. (2010). Forbidden language: A brief history of U.S. language policy. In P. Gándara & M. Hopkins (Eds.), *Forbidden language: English learners and restrictive language policies* (pp. 20–36). New York: Teachers College Press.

Gándara, P., & Maxwell-Jolly, J. (2006). Critical issues in developing the teacher corps for English learners. In K. Téllez, & H. Waxman (Eds.), *Preparing quality educators for English language learners: Research, policies, and practices* (pp. 99–120). Mahwah, NJ: Erlbaum.

Gándara, P., Maxwell-Jolly, J., & Driscoll, A. (2005). *Listening to teachers of English language learners: A survey of California teachers' challenges, experiences, and professional development needs.* Retrieved from http://www.cftl.org/Our_Publications.htm

Garan, E. (2002). Beyond the smoke and mirrors: A critique of the national reading report on phonics. In R. Allington (Ed.), *Big brother and the national reading curriculum: How ideology trumped evidence* (pp. 90–111). Portsmouth, NH: Heinemann.

Garan, E. (2004). *In defense of our children: When politics, profit, and education collide.* Portsmouth, NH: Heinemann.

García, E., Arias, M. B., Murri, N. H., & Serna, C. (2010). Developing responsive teachers: A challenge for a demographic reality. *Journal of Teacher Education, 61*(1–2), 132–142.

García, E., & Cuéllar, D. (2006). Who are these linguistically and culturally diverse students? *Teachers College Record, 108*(11), 2220–2246.

García, G. E., McKoon, G., & August, D. (2006a). Synthesis: Language and literacy assessment. In D. August & T. Shanahan (Eds.), *Developing literacy in second-language learners: Report of the National Literacy Panel on Language Minority Children and Youth* (pp. 583–596). Mahwah, NJ: Erlbaum.

García, G. E., McKoon, G., & August, D. (2006b). Language and literacy assessment of language-minority students. In D. August & T. Shanahan (Eds.), *Developing literacy in second-language learners: Report of the National Literacy Panel on Language Minority Children and Youth* (pp. 597–624). Mahwah, NJ: Erlbaum.

García, E., & Stritikus, T. (2006). Prop 227 in California: Issues for the preparation of quality teachers for linguistically and culturally diverse students. In K. Téllez & H. Waxman (Eds.), *Preparing quality educators for English language learners: Research, policies, and practices* (pp. 45–69). Mahwah, NJ: Erlbaum.

Gay, G. (2000). *Culturally responsive teaching: Theory, research, and practice.* New York: Teachers College Press.

Genesee, F., Lindholm-Leary, K., Saunders, W., & Christian, D. (2005). English language learners in U.S. schools: An overview of research findings. *Journal of Education for Students Placed at Risk, 10*(4), 363–385.

Genesee, F., Lindholm-Leary, K., Saunders, W., & Christian, D. (Eds.). (2006). *Educating English language learners: A synthesis of research evidence.* New York: Cambridge University Press.

Genishi, C., & Dyson, A. H. (2009). *Children, language, and literacy: Diverse learners in diverse times.* New York: Teachers College Press.

Gersten, R. (1999). Lost opportunities: Challenges confronting four teachers of English-language learners. *Elementary School Journal, 100*(1), 37–56.

Gibson, M. A., Gándara, P., & Koyama, J. P. (Eds.). (2004). *School connections: U.S. Mexican youth, peers, and school achievement.* New York: Teachers College Press.

Goertz, M., Oláh, L., & Riggan, M. (2009). *Can interim assessments be used for instructional change?* Retrieved from the Consortium for Policy Research in Education website: www.cpre.org

Goldenberg, C. (2008). Teaching English language learners: What the research does—and does not—say. *American Educator, 32*(2), 8–44.

Goldenberg, C., & Coleman, R. (2010). *Promoting academic achievement among English learners: A guide to the research.* Thousand Oaks, CA: Corwin Press.

Goldenberg, C. & Gallimore, R. (1995). Immigrant Latino parents' values and beliefs about their children's education: Continuities and discontinuities across cultures and generations. In P. Pintrich & M. Maehr (Eds.), *Advances in achievement and motivation* (Vol. 9, pp. 183–227). Greenwich, CT: JAI Press.

Goldenberg, C., Gallimore, R., Reese, L., & Garnier, H. (2001). Cause or effect? A longitudinal study of immigrant Latino parents' aspirations and expectations, and their children's school performance. *American Educational Research Journal, 38*(3), 547–582.

Gonzáles, N., Moll, L., & Amanti, C. (2005). *Funds of knowledge: Theorizing practices in households and classrooms.* Mahwah, NJ: Erlbaum.

Gonzales, R. (2008). Born in the shadows: The uncertain futures of the children of unauthorized Mexican migrants (unpublished Ph.D. thesis). University of California, Irvine, CA.

Goodman, Y. (2003). Informal methods of evaluation. In J. Flood, D. Lapp, J. Squire, & J. Jensen (Eds.), *Handbook of research on teaching the English language arts* (pp. 600–607). Mahwah, NJ: Erlbaum.

Gorski, P. (2006, February 9). The classist underpinnings of Ruby Payne's framework. *Teachers College Record.* Retrieved from http://www.tcrecord.org ID Number: 12322

Guaglianone, C., Payne, M., Kinsey, G., & Chiero, R. (2009). Teaching performance assessment: A comparative study of implementation and impact among California state university campuses. *Issues in Teacher Education, 18*(1), 129–148.

Gude, O. (2009). Art education for democratic life. *Art Education, 62*(6), 6–11.

Gunderson, L. (2009). *ESL (ELL) literacy instruction: A guidebook to theory and practice* (2nd ed.). New York: Routledge.

Guèvremont, A., Roos, N., & Brownell, M. (2007). Predictors and consequences of grade retention: Examining data from Manitoba, Canada. *Canadian Journal of School Psychology, 22*(1), 50–67.

Gutiérrez, K., & Orellana, M. (2006). At last: The "problem" of English learners: Constructing genres of difference. *Research in the Teaching of English, 40*(4), 502–507.

Haager, D., Klingner, J., & Vaughn, S. (Eds.). (2007). *Evidence-based reading practices for response to intervention.* Baltimore, MD: Brookes Publishing.

Haberman, M. (1996). The pedagogy of poverty vs. good teaching. In W. Ayers & P. Ford (Eds.), *City kids, city teachers* (pp. 118–130). New York: The New Press.

Hakuta, K., Butler, Y. G., & Witt, D. (2000). *How long does it take English learners to attain proficiency?* Santa Barbara: University of California Linguistic Minority Research Institute.

Haladyna, T. M. (2002). *Essentials of standardized achievement testing: Validity and accountability.* Boston: Allyn & Bacon.

Hammerness, K., Darling-Hammond, L., Grossman, P., Rust, F., & Shulman, L. (2005). The design of teacher education programs. In L. Darling-Hammond & J. Bransford (Eds.), *Preparing teachers for a changing world: What teachers should learn and be able to do* (pp. 390–441). San Francisco: Jossey-Bass.

Haskins, R., & Rouse, C. (2005). *Closing achievement gaps. The future of children policy brief.* Washington, DC: The Future of Children.

Hernandez, D. J., Denton, N. A., & Macartney, S. E. (2007). Young Hispanic children in the 21st century. *Journal of Latinos & Education, 6*(3), 209–228.

Herrera, S. (2010). *Biography-driven culturally responsive teaching.* New York: Teachers College Press.

Hill, M., & Vasudevan, L. (Eds.). (2007). *Media, learning, and sites of possibility.* New York: Peter Lang.

Ho, A. D. (2008). The problem with "proficiency": Limitations of statistics and policy under No Child Left Behind. *Educational Researcher, 37*(6), 351–360.

Hoffman, J., Paris, S., Salas, R., Patterson, E. & Assaf, L. (2003). High-stakes assessment in the language arts: The piper plays, the players dance, but who pays the price? In J. Flood, D. Lapp, J. Squire, & J. Jensen (Eds.), *Handbook of research on teaching the English language arts* (pp. 619–630). Mahwah, NJ: Erlbaum.

Hondagneu-Sotelo, P. (2006). *Gendered transitions: Mexican experiences of immigration.* Berkeley: University of California Press.

Hondagneu-Sotelo, P., & Ávila, E. (1997). "I'm here, but I'm there": The meanings of Latina transnational motherhood. *Gender & Society, 11*(5), 548–571.

Houghton Mifflin. (2003). *Houghton Mifflin Reading: A legacy of literacy.* Boston: Author.

Hudelson, S. (1994). Literacy development of second language children. In F. Genesee (Ed.), *Educating second language children* (pp. 129–57). New York: Cambridge University Press.

Hull, G. A., Stornaiuolo, A., & Sahni, U. (2010). Cultural citizenship and cosmopolitan practice: Global youth communicate online. *English Education, 24*(4), 331–367.

Hunter, M. (1983). *Enhancing teaching.* Upper Saddle River, NJ: Prentice Hall.

Irvine, P., & Larson, J. (2001). Literacy packages in practice: Constructing academic disadvantage. In J. Larson (Ed.), *Literacy as snake oil: Beyond the quick fix* (pp. 45–70). New York: Peter Lang.

Jaeger, E. (2006). Silencing teachers in an era of scripted reading. *Rethinking Schools, 20*(3), 39–41.

Janks, H., & Comber, B. (2005). Critical literacy across continents. In K. Pahl & J. Rowsell (Eds.), *Travel notes from the new literacy studies* (pp. 95–117). Tonawanda, NY: Multilingual Matters.

Johnson, E., Mellard, D. F., Fuchs, D., & McKnight, M. A. (2006). *Responsiveness to intervention (RTI): How to do it.* Lawrence, KS: National Research Center on Learning Disabilities.

Kao, G., & Tienda, M. (2005). Optimism and achievement: The educational performance of immigrant youth. In M. Suárez-Orozco, C. Suárez-Orozco, & D. Qin (Eds.), *The new immigration: An interdisciplinary reader* (pp. 331–344). New York: Routledge.

Kersten, J., & Pardo, L. (2007). Finessing and hybridizing: Innovative literacy practices in Reading First classrooms. *The Reading Teacher 61*(2), 146–154.

Kieffer, M., Lesaux, N., Rivera, M., & Francis, D. (2009). Accommodations for English language learners taking large-scale assessments: A meta-analysis on effectiveness and validity. *Review of Educational Research, 79*(3), 1168–1201.

Knight, S., & Wiseman, D. (2006). Lessons learned from a research synthesis on the effects of teachers' professional development on culturally diverse students. In K. Téllez & H. Waxman (Eds.), *Preparing quality educators for English language learners: Research, policies, and practices* (pp. 71–98). Mahwah, NJ: Erlbaum.

Kornfeld, J., Grady, K., Marker, P., & Ruddell, M. (2007). Caught in the current: A self-study of state-mandated compliance in a teacher education program. *Teachers College Record, 109*(8), 1902–1930.

Kozol, J. (2007, September 10). Why I am fasting: An explanation to my friends. *Huffington Post.* Retrieved from http://www.huffingtonpost.com/jonathan-kozol/why-i-am-fasting-an-expla_b_63622.html

Krashen, S. D. (1985). *The input hypothesis: Issues and implications.* London: Longman.

Krashen, S. (2002). More smoke and mirrors: A critique of the national reading panel report on fluency. In R. Allington (Ed.), *Big brother and the national reading curriculum: How ideology trumped evidence* (pp. 112–124). Portsmouth, NH: Heinemann.

Labaree, D. F. (2006). *The trouble with ed schools.* New Haven, CT: Yale University Press.

Lagemann, E. C. (2000). *An elusive science: The troubling history of education research.* Chicago: The University of Chicago Press.

Lam, W. S. E. (2000). Second language literacy and the design of the self: A case study of a teenager writing on the internet. *TESOL Quarterly, 34*(3), 457–482.

Lam, W. S. E. (2005). Second language socialization in a bilingual chat room. *Language Learning and Technology, 8*(3), 44–65.

Lantolf, J. P., & Frawley, W. (1988). Proficiency: Understanding the construct. *Studies in Second Language Acquisition, 10*(2), 181–195.

Larson, J. (2009). New literacy studies: Literacy learning through a sociocultural lens. In C. Compton-Lilly (Ed.), *Breaking the silence: Recognizing the social and cultural resources students bring to the classroom* (pp. 13–23). Newark, NJ: International Reading Association.

Lee, S. (1994). Behind the model-minority stereotype: Voices of high- and low-achieving Asian American students. *Anthropology & Education Quarterly, 25*(4), 413–429.

Lee, S. K., Ajayi, L., & Richards, R. (2007). Teachers' perceptions of the efficacy of the Open Court program for English proficient and English language learners. *Teacher Education Quarterly,* Summer, 19–33.

Lesaux, N., Geva, E., Koda, K., Siegel, L., & Shanahan, T. (2008). Development of literacy in second-language learners. In D. August & T. Shanahan (Eds.), *Developing reading and writing in second-language learners* (pp. 27–60). New York: Routledge.

Linton, A., & Franklin, R. (2010). Bilingualism for the children: Dual-language programs under restrictive language policies. In P. Gándara & M. Hopkins (Eds.), *Forbidden language: English learners and restrictive language policies* (pp. 175–191). New York: Teachers College Press.

Llosa, L. (2007). Validating a standards-based classroom assessment of English proficiency: A multitrait-multimethod approach. *Language Testing, 24*(4), 489–515.

Lucas, T. & Grinberg, J. (2008). Responding to the linguistic reality of mainstream classrooms: Preparing all teachers to teach English language learners. In M. Cochran-Smith, S. Feiman-Nemser, & J. McIntyre (Eds.), *Handbook of research on teacher education: Enduring issues in changing contexts* (3rd ed.; pp. 606–636). Mahwah, NJ: Erlbaum.

Lucas, T., Villegas, A. M., & Freedson-Gonzalez, M. (2008). Linguistically responsive teacher education: Preparing classroom teachers to teach English language learners. *Journal of Teacher Education, 59*(4), 361–373.

Luke, A. (1988). *Literacy, textbooks, and ideology: Postwar literacy instruction and the mythology of Dick and Jane.* New York: Falmer Press.

Marzano, R. (2006). *Classroom assessment & grading that work.* Alexandria, VA: Association for Supervision and Curriculum Development.

McCarthey, S. (2009). The impact of No Child Left Behind on teachers' writing instruction. *Written Communication, 25*(4), 462–505.

McRae, D. (2002). Test score gains for Open Court schools in California: Results from three cohorts of schools. Retrieved from http://www.sraonline.com/index.php/home/ocrr/1115

Medina, J. (2010). Standards raised, more students fail tests. *The New York Times.* Retrieved from http://www.nytimes.com/2010/07/29/education/29scores.html

Menard-Warwick, J. (2007). Biliteracy and schooling in an extended-family Nicaraguan immigrant household: The sociohistorical construction of parental involvement. *Anthropology & Education Quarterly, 38*(2), 119–137.

Menken, K. (2006). Teaching to the test: How No Child Left Behind impacts language policy, curriculum, and instruction for English language learners. *Bilingual Research Journal, 30*(2), 521–546.

Menken, K. (2008). *English learners left behind: Standardized testing as language policy.* Clevedon, UK: Multilingual Matters Ltd.

Menken, K., & Antunez, B. (2001). *An overview of the preparation and certification of teachers working with limited English proficient (LEP) students.* Washington, DC: National Clearinghouse for Bilingual Education.

Milanowski, A. T., Kimball, S. M., & White, B. (2004). *The relationship between standards-based teacher evaluation scores and student achievement: Replication and extensions at three sites.* University of Wisconsin-Madison: Consortium for Policy Research in Education.

Milk, R., Mercado, D., & Sapiens, A. (1992). Rethinking the education of teachers of language minority children: Developing reflective teachers for changing schools. *NCBE FOCUS: Occasional Papers in Bilingual Education, 6.* Retrieved from http://ncela.edstudies.net/pubs/focus/focus6.htm

Millman, J. (2009, Fall). Critical literacy and art education: Alternatives in the school reform movement. *Perspectives on Urban Education, 6*(2), 68–71.

Monzó, L., & Rueda, R. (2009). Passing for English fluent: Latino immigrant children masking language proficiency. *Anthropology & Education Quarterly, 40*(1), 20–40.

Morales, P. Z., & Aldana, U. (2010). Learning in two languages: Programs with political promise. In P. Gándara & M. Hopkins (Eds.), *Forbidden language: English learners and restrictive language policies* (pp. 159–174). New York: Teachers College Press.

Morrell, E. (2008). *Critical literacy and urban youth: Pedagogies of access, dissent, and liberation.* New York: Routledge.

Morse, S., & Ludovina, F. (1999). *Responding to undocumented children in the schools* (No. EDO-RC-99–1). Charleston, WV: ERIC Clearinghouse on Rural Education and Small Schools.

Moskin, M. (1971). *Toto.* New York: Coward, McCann & Geoghegan.

Moustafa, M., & Land, R. (2002). The reading achievement of socioeconomically-disadvantaged children in urban schools using Open Court vs. comparably disadvantaged children in urban schools using non-scripted reading programs. *Urban Learning, Teaching, and Research Annual Yearbook,* 44–53.

Murnane, R., & Cohen, D. (1986). Merit pay and the evaluation problem: Why most merit pay plans fail and a few survive. *Harvard Educational Review, 56*(1), 1–17.

Nation, I. S. P. (2009). *Teaching ESL/EFL reading and writing.* New York: Routledge.

National Center for Education Statistics. (2009a). *Report cards provided by the state, student-performance data included in report cards, graduation or drop-out rates included in high school report cards, and the presence of student identification systems, by state: 2005–06* (Table 1.1). Retrieved from http://nces.ed.gov/programs/statereform/tab1_1.asp

National Center for Education Statistics. (2009b). *State-reported elements of longitudinal data systems, by state: 2008–09* (Table 1.6). Retrieved from http://nces.ed.gov/programs/statereform/tab1_6.asp

National Center for Education Statistics. (2009c). *Percent of all schools not making Adequate Yearly Progress, and percent of all schools identified as in need of improvement, by state: 2006–07* (Table 1.2). Retrieved from http://nces.ed.gov/programs/statereform/tab1_2.asp#f5/

National Reading Panel. (2000). *Teaching children to read: An evidence-based assessment of the scientific research literature and its implications for reading instruction.* Washington, DC: National Institute of Child Health and Human Development.

Nazario, S. (2007). *Enrique's journey.* New York: Random House.

Nichols, S. (2006). From boardroom to classroom: Tracing a globalised discourse on thinking through internet texts and teaching practices. In K. Pahl & J. Rowsell (Eds.), *Travel notes from the new literacy studies: Instances of practice* (pp. 173–194). Clevedon, UK: Multilingual Matters.

No Child Left Behind Act of 2001, 107th Congress. (January 8, 2002).

Nystrand, M., Gamoran, A., Kachur, R., & Prendergast, C. (1997). *Opening dialogue: Understanding the dynamics of language and learning in the English classroom.* New York: Teachers College Press.

Oakes, J. (1986). *Keeping track: How schools structure inequality.* New Haven, CT: Yale University Press.

O'Brien, R. (1971). *Mrs. Frisby and the rats of Nimh.* New York: Atheneum.

Ogbu, J. U. (1991). Immigrant and involuntary minorities in comparative perspective. In M. Gibson & J. Ogbu (Eds.), *Minority status and schooling: A comparative study of immigrant and involuntary minorities* (pp. 3–36). New York: Garland.

Okhremtchouk, I., Seiki, S., Gilliland, B., Ateh, C., Wallace, M., & Kato, A. (2009). Voices of pre-service teachers: Perspectives on the performance assessment for California teachers (PACT). *Issues in Teacher Education, 18*(1), 39–62.

Olmedo, I. (2003). Accommodation and resistance: Latinas struggle for their children's education. *Anthropology & Education Quarterly, 34*(4), 373–395.

Olneck, M. R. (2009). What have immigrants wanted from American schools? What do they want now? Historical and contemporary perspectives on immigrants, language, and American schooling. *American Journal of Education, 115*(3), 379–406.

Olsen, L. (1997). *Made in America: Immigrant students in our public schools.* New York: The New Press.

Olsen, L. (2000). Learning English and learning America: Immigrants in the center of a storm. *Theory into Practice, 39*(4), 196.

Orellana, M., & Gutiérrez, K. (2006). At last: What's the problem? Constructing different genres for the study of English learners. *Research in the Teaching of English, 41*(1), 118–123.

Organisation for Economic Cooperation and Development. (2007). *PISA 2006: Science competencies for tomorrow's world executive summary.* Paris: Author.

Palmer, D., & García, E. (2000). Voices from the field: Bilingual educators speak candidly about Proposition 227. *Bilingual Research Journal, 24* (1&2), 169–178.

Paris, S., Lawton, T., Turner, J., & Roth, J. (1991). Developmental perspective on standardized achievement testing. *Educational Researcher, 20*(5), 12–20.

Paris, S. (2005). Reinterpreting the development of reading skills. *Reading Research Quarterly, 40*(2), 184–202.

Parks, R., & Haskins, J. (1992). *Rosa Parks: My story.* New York: Penguin Putnam.

Parrish, T. B., Merickel, A., Pérez, M., Linquanti, R., Socias, M., Spain, A., Speroni, C., Esra, P., Brock, L., & Delancey, D. (2006). *Effects of the implementation of Proposition 227 on the education of English learners, K–12: Findings from a five-year evaluation.* Palo Alto: American Institutes for Research & WestEd.

Passel, J. (2005). *Unauthorized migrants: Numbers and characteristics.* Washington, DC: Pew Hispanic Center. Retrieved from http://pewhispanic.org/reports/

Passel, J., & Cohn, D. (2008). *Trends in unauthorized immigration: Undocumented inflow now trails legal inflow.* Washington, DC: Pew Hispanic Center. Retrieved from http://pewhispanic.org/reports/.

Paugh, P., Carey, J., King-Jackson, V., & Russell, S. (2007). Negotiating the literacy block: Constructing spaces for critical literacy in a high-stakes setting. *Language Arts, 85*(1), 31–42.

Payne, R. (2001). *A framework for understanding poverty.* Highlands, TX: Aha! Process.

Pearson, P. D. (2000). Reading in the 20th century. In T. Good (Ed.), *American education: Yesterday, today, and tomorrow* (pp. 152–208). Chicago: University of Chicago Press.

Pearson, P. D. (2004). The reading wars. *Educational Policy, 18*(1), 216–252.

Pearson, P. D. (2010). Reading first: Hard to live with—or without. *Journal of Literacy Research, 42*(1), 100–108.

Pearson, P. D., & Hiebert, E. (2010). National reports in literacy: Building a scientific based for practice and policy. *Educational Researcher, 39*(4), 286–294.

Pease-Alvarez, L., & Samway, K. D. (2008). Negotiating a top-down reading program mandate: The experiences of one school. *Language Arts, 86*(1), 32–41.

Pecheone, R., & Chung, R. R. (2006). Evidence in teacher education: The performance assessment for California teachers (PACT). *Journal of Teacher Education, 57*(1), 22–36.

Pecheone, R., & Stansbury, K. (1996). Connecting teacher assessment and school reform. *The Elementary School Journal, 97*(2), 163–77.

Peck, C., Gallucci, C., & Sloan, T. (2010). Negotiating implementation of high-stakes performance assessment policies in teacher education: From compliance to inquiry. *Journal of Teacher Education, 61*(5), 451–463.

Pedulla, J., Abrams, L., Madaus, G., Russell, M., Ramos, M., & Miao, J. (2003). *Perceived effects of state-mandated testing programs on teaching and learning: Findings from a national survey of teachers.* Boston, MA: National Board on Educational Testing and Policy.

Pennington, J. (2004). *The colonization of literacy education: A story of reading in one elementary school.* New York: Peter Lang.

Perlstein, L. (2007). *Tested: One American school struggles to make the grade.* New York: Henry Holt & Co.

Perryman, J. (2006). Panoptic performativity and school inspection regimes: Disciplinary mechanisms and life under special measures. *Journal of Education Policy, 21*(2), 147–161.

Popham, J. (2008). *Transformative assessment.* Alexandria, VA: Association for Curriculum Supervision and Development.

Portes, A., & Rumbaut, R. (2006). *Immigrant America: A portrait* (3rd ed.). Berkeley, CA: University of California Press.

Powers, D. L. (2010). *Teachers' perceptions of the effects of No Child Left Behind on classroom instruction: A cross case analysis applying Dewey's theory of instructional methods* (Unpublished Ed.D. thesis). California State University, Long Beach, Long Beach, CA.

Pressley, M. (2006). *Reading instruction that works: The case for balanced teaching.* New York: Guilford Press.

Ranker, J. (2006). "There's fire magic, electric magic, ice magic, or poison magic": The world of video games and Adrian's compositions about Gauntlet Legends. *Language Arts, 84*(1), 21–33.

Ravitch, D. (2010). *The death and life of the American school system: How testing and choice are undermining education.* New York: Basic Books.

Reese, L. (2002). Parental strategies in contrasting cultural settings: Families in Mexico and "el Norte." *Anthropology & Education Quarterly, 33*(1), 30–59.

Rinke, C., & Valli, L. (2010). Making adequate yearly progress: Teacher learning in school-based accountability contexts. *Teachers College Record, 112*(3), 645–684.

Roderick, M. R., & Nagaoka, J. (2005). Retention under Chicago's high-stakes testing program: Helpful, harmful, or harmless? *Educational Evaluation and Policy Analysis, 27*(4), 309–340.

Rogers, R., Mosely, M., & Folkes, A. (2009). Standing up to neoliberalism through critical literacy education. *Language Arts, 87*(2), 127–138.

Ruiz, N., & Morales-Ellis, L. (2005). "Gracias por la oportunidad, pero voy a buscar otro trabajo…" A beginning teacher resists high-stakes curriculum. In B. Altwerger (Ed.), *Reading for profit: How the bottom line leaves kids behind* (pp. 199–215). Portsmouth, NH: Heinemann.

Rujumba, K. (2010, June 15). Pittsburgh board, teachers OK pact. *The Pittsburgh Post-Gazette.* Retrieved from http://www.post-gazette.com/pg/10166/1065651-298.stm

Sakurai, G. (1995). *Mae Jemison: Space scientist.* New York: Scholastic.

Salomone, R. (2010). *True American: Language, identity, and the education of immigrant children.* Cambridge, MA: Harvard University Press.

Samuels, S. J. (2007). Commentary: The DIBELS test is speed of barking at print: What we mean by reading fluency. *Reading Research Quarterly, 42*(4), 563–566.

Samway, K. D. (2006). *When English language learners write: Connecting research to practice, K-8.* Portsmouth, NH: Heinemann.

Samway, K. D., & Pease-Alvarez, L. (2005). Teachers' perspectives on Open Court. In B. Altwerger (Ed.), *Reading for profit: How the bottom line leaves kids behind* (pp. 142–155). Portsmouth, NH: Heinemann.

Samway, K. D., & Taylor, D. (2008). *Teaching English language learners: Strategies that work.* New York: Scholastic.

Schemo, D., & Fessenden, F. (2003, December 3). A miracle revisited: Measuring success; Gains in Houston schools: How real are they? *The New York Times*. Retrieved from http://www.nytimes.com/2003/12/03/us/a-miracle-revisited-measuring-success-gains-in-houston-schools-how-real-are-they.html?scp=1&sq =texas+rod+paige+score+test&st=nyt

Senate Bill (SB) 2042, California State Legislature. (1998, September 18). Retrieved from http://leginfo.ca.gov/cgi-bin/postquery?bill_number=sb_2042 &sess=9798&house=B&author=alpert

Senate Bill (SB) 1209, California State Legislature. (2006, September 28). Retrieved from http://leginfo.ca.gov/cgi-bin/postquery?bill_number=sb_1209&sess= 0506& house=B&author=scott

Shanahan, T., & Beck, I. (2006). Effective literacy teaching for English-language learners. In D. August & T. Shanahan (Eds.), *Developing literacy in second-language learners: Report of the National Literacy Panel on Language Minority Children and Youth* (pp. 415–488). Mahwah, NJ: Erlbaum.

Shannon, P. (1989). *Broken promises: Reading instruction in twentieth-century America*. Granby, MA: Bergin & Garvey.

Shelton, N. (2005). First do no harm: Teachers' reactions to mandated Reading Mastery. In B. Altwerger (Ed.), *Reading for profit: How the bottom line leaves kids behind* (pp. 184–198). Portsmouth, NH: Heinemann.

Shin, F. (2004). English language development standards and benchmarks: Policy issues and a call for more focused research. *Bilingual Research Journal, 28*(2), 253–266.

Skindrud, K., & Gersten, R. (2006). An evaluation of two contrasting approaches for improving reading achievement in a large urban district. *Elementary School Journal, 106*(5), 389–407.

Skoll, J., Weyerman, D. (Producers), & Guggenheim, D. (2010). *Waiting for Superman* [Motion picture]. Beverly Hills, CA: Participant Media.

Slavin, R., Lake, C., Chambers, B., Cheung, A., & Davis, S. (2009). Effective reading programs for the elementary grades: A best-evidence synthesis. *Review of Educational Research, 79*(4), 1391–1466.

Slavin, R. E., Madden, N. A., Chambers, B., & Haxby, B. (2009). *Two million children: Success for All*. Thousand Oaks, CA: Corwin.

Smith, K., & McKnight, K. S. (2009). Remembering to laugh and explore: Improvisational activities for literacy teaching in urban classrooms. *International Journal of Education & the Arts, 10*(12). Retrieved from http://www.ijea.org/v10n12/

Snow, C., & Fillmore, L.W. (2000). *What teachers need to know about language*. Washington, DC: Center for Applied Linguistics.

Snyder, J. (2009). Taking stock of performance assessments in teaching. *Issues in Teacher Education, 18*(1), 7–12.

Solórzano, R. (2008). High stakes testing: Issues, implications, and remedies for English Language Learners. *Review of Educational Research, 78*(2), 260–329.

Special Education Reading Task Force, California Department of Education, & California State Board of Education. (1999). *The California reading initiative and special education in California*. Sacramento: California Department of Education. Retrieved from http://www.calstat.org/publications/pdfs/ca_reading_initiative.pdf

SRA/McGraw-Hill. (2000). *Open Court Reading*. Columbus, OH: Author.

SRA/McGraw-Hill. (2002). *Open Court Reading: Teacher's Edition, Level 4, Unit 1*. Columbus, OH: Author.

Stevens, L. P., & Bean, T. (2007). *Critical literacy*. Thousand Oaks, CA: Sage.

Stritikus, T. (2002). *Immigrant children and the politics of English-only: Views from the classroom*. New York: LFB Scholarly.

Suárez-Orozco, C. (2005). Identities under siege: Immigration stress and social mirroring among the children of immigrants. In M. Suárez-Orozco, C. Suárez-Orozco, & D. Qin (Eds.), *The new immigration: An interdisciplinary reader* (pp. 135–156). New York: Brunner-Routledge.

Suárez-Orozco, C., & Suárez-Orozco, M. (2002). *Children of immigration*. Cambridge, MA: Harvard University Press.

Suárez-Orozco, C., & Suárez-Orozco, M. (2009). Educating Latino immigrant students in the twenty-first century: Principles for the Obama administration. *Harvard Educational Review, 79*(2), 327–340.

Suárez-Orozco, M., Suárez-Orozco, C., & Todorova, I. (2008). *Learning in a new land: Immigrant students in American society*. Cambridge, MA: Harvard University Press.

Suárez-Orozco, C. & Todorova, I. (Eds.). (2003). *Understanding the social worlds of immigrant youth*. San Francisco: Jossey-Bass.

Sunderman, G., Kim, J. S., & Orfield, G. (2005). *NCLB meets school realities: Lessons from the field*. Thousand Oaks, CA: Corwin Press.

Swartz, J., & Johnston, K. (2003). *Efficacy study of Houghton Mifflin reading: A legacy of literacy*. Cambridge, MA: Abt Associates.

Sweeney, J. (1998). *Me on the map*. New York: Dragonfly Books.

Takanishi, R. (2004). Leveling the playing field: Supporting immigrant children from birth to eight. *The Future of Children, 14*(2), 61–79.

Téllez, K., & Waxman, H. (2006). Preparing quality teachers for English language learners: An overview of the critical issues. In K. Téllez & H. Waxman (Eds.), *Preparing quality educators for English language learners: Research, policies, and practices* (pp. 1–22). Mahwah, NJ: Erlbaum.

Thinking Maps, Inc. (2004). *Thinking Maps*. Cary, NC: Innovative learning Group.

Toch, T. (2006). *Margins of error: The education testing industry in the No Child Left Behind era*. Washington, DC: Education Sector.

Torgerson, C., Macy, S., Beare, P., & Tanner, D. (2009). Fresno assessment of student teachers: A teacher performance assessment that informs practice. *Issues in Teacher Education, 18*(1), 63–82.

Turque, B. (2009, April 7). Rhee works on overhaul of teacher evaluations. *The Washington Post*. Retrieved from http://www.washingtonpost.com/wp-dyn/content/article/2009/04/06/AR2009040603600.html?sid=ST2009091001966

Turque, B. (2010, July 24). Rhee dismisses 241 D.C. teachers; union vows to contest firings. *The Washington Post*. Retrieved from http://www.washingtonpost.com/wp-dyn/content/article/2010/07/23/AR2010072303093.html

Tyack, D. (2003). *Seeking common ground: Public schools in a diverse society*. Cambridge, MA: Harvard University Press.

Urbina, I. (2010, January 11). As school exit tests prove tough, states ease standards. *The New York Times*. Retrieved from http://www.nytimes.com/2010/01/12/education/12exit.html?ref=no_child_left_behind_act

U.S. Department of Education. (2003). *Title I, Standards and assessment, non-regulatory draft guidance*. Retrieved from www2.ed.gov/policy/elsec/guid/saaguidance03.doc

U.S. Department of Education. (2010). *Race to the top fund.* Retrieved from http://www2.ed.gov/programs/racetothetop/index.html

Valdés, G. (1996). *Con respeto: Bridging the distance between culturally diverse families and schools.* New York: Teachers College Press.

Valdés, G. (2001). *Learning and not learning English: Latino students in American schools.* New York: Teachers College Press.

Valenzuela, A. (1999). *Subtractive schooling: U. S.-Mexican youth and the politics of caring.* Albany: The State University of New York Press.

Valli, L., & Buese, D. (2007). The changing role of teachers in an era of high-stakes accountability. *American Educational Research Journal, 44*(3), 519–558.

Valli, L., & Chambliss, M. (2007). Creating classroom cultures: One teacher, two lessons, and a high-stakes test. *Anthropology & Education Quarterly, 38*(1), 57–75.

Valli, L., Croninger, R., Chambliss, M., Graeber, A. & Buesi, D. (2008). *Test-driven: High-stakes accountability in elementary schools.* New York: Teachers College Press.

Vinovskis, M. (2009). *From A Nation at Risk to No Child Left Behind: National education goals and the creation of federal education policy.* New York: Teachers College Press.

Vygotsky, L. (1978). *Mind in society.* Cambridge, MA: Harvard University Press.

Walpole, S., & McKenna, M. (2007). *Differentiated reading instruction: Strategies for the primary grades.* New York and London: The Guilford Press.

Walqui, A., Koelsch, N., Hamburger, L., Gaarder, D., Insaurralde, A., Schmida, M., Weiss, S., & Estrada, P. (2010). *What are we doing to middle school English learners? Findings and recommendations for change from a study of California EL programs (research report).* San Francisco: WestEd.

Ware, P. D. (2008). Language learners and multimedia literacy in and after school. *Pedagogies: An International Journal, 3*(1), 37–51.

Ware, P. D., & Warschauer, M. (2005). Hybrid literacy texts and practices in technology-intensive environments. *International Journal of Educational Research, 43*(7–8), 432-445.

Warren, J. R., & Grodsky, E. (2009). Exit exams harm students who fail them—and don't benefit students who pass them. *Phi Delta Kappan, 90*(9), 645–649.

Weinstein, C., Taumlinson-Clarke, S., & Curran, M. (2004). Toward a conception of culturally responsive classroom management. *Journal of Teacher Education, 55*(1), 25–38.

Weinstein, R. (2002). *Reaching higher: The power of expectation of schooling.* Cambridge, MA: Harvard University Press.

Welner, K. (2004). *Legal rights: The overrepresentation of culturally and linguistically diverse students in special education.* Retrieved from National Center for Culturally Responsive Educational Systems website: http://www.nccrest.org/publications/briefs.html: NCCREST/

Wiley, T., & Wright, W. (2004). Against the undertow: Language-minority education policy and politics in the "age of accountability." *Educational Policy, 18*(1), 142–168. doi: 10.1177/0895904803260030

Wiltz, N., & Wilson, G. P. (2006). An inquiry into children's reading in one urban school using SRA Reading Mastery (direct instruction). *Journal of Literacy Research, 37*(4), 493–528.

Working Group on ELL Policy. (2010). *Improving educational outcomes for English language learners: Recommendations for the reauthorization of the elementary and secondary education act.* Retrieved from http://ellpolicy.org/esea/

Wright, W. (2002). The effects of high stakes testing in an inner-city elementary school: The curriculum, the teachers, and the English language learners. *Current Issues in Education, 5*(5). Retrieved from http://cie.asu.edu/volume5/number5/

Wright, W. (2005). English language learners left behind in Arizona: The nullification of accommodations in the intersection of federal and state policies. *Bilingual Research Journal, 29*(1), 1–29.

Wright, W. (2006). A catch-22 for language learners. *Educational Leadership, 64*(3), 22–27.

Wright, W. (2010). *Foundations for teaching English language learners: Research, theory, policy, and practice.* Philadelphia, PA: Caslon Publishing.

Wyse, D., & Styles, M. (2007). Synthetic phonics and the teaching of reading: The debate surrounding England's "Rose report." *Literacy, 41*(1), 35–42.

Xu, S. H. (2010). *Teaching English language learners: Literacy strategies and resources for K-6.* New York: The Guilford Press.

Yatvin, J. (2002). Babes in the woods: The wanderings of the national reading panel. In R. Allington (Ed.), *Big brother and the national reading curriculum: How ideology trumped evidence* (pp. 125–136). Portsmouth, NH: Heinemann.

Zacher Pandya, J. (forthcoming. 2012a). Mandating and standardizing the teaching of critical literacy skills: A cautionary tale. *Theory Into Practice.*

Zacher Pandya, J. (forthcoming, 2012b). A Scale Analysis of the Effects of US Federal Policy. *Pedagogies: An International Journal.* Accepted for publication 2011.

Zavis, A., & Barboza, T. (2010, September 28). Teacher's suicide shocks schools. *The Los Angeles Times.* Retrieved from http://articles.latimes.com/2010/sep/28/local/la-me-south-gate-teacher-20100928.

Zellmer, M., Frontier, A., & Pheifer, D. (2006). What are NCLB's instructional costs? *Educational Leadership, 64*(3), 43–46.

Zimmerman, J. (2010). What are schools for? *The New York Review of Books, 57*(15), 29–31.

Zlolniski, C. (2006). *Janitors, street vendors, and activists: The lives of Mexican immigrants in Silicon Valley.* Berkeley: University of California Press.

Index

Abedi, J., 10, 13n1, 20, 69n7, 74, 101, 103
Abrams, L., 17, 74, 81
Academic abilities, 28
Academic Performance Index (API), 2, 14, 18
Accessibility, of texts used in tests, 22
Accountability. *See also* No Child Left Behind (NCLB)
  in elementary schools, 14–17
  high-volume, high-stakes testing and, 2–3
  learning and, 105–6
  new teachers and, 79–95
  pressures created by, 20–21, 26–27
  teacher education in context of, 94–95
  test-based approach to, ix–x
Adequate Yearly Progress (AYP), 14, 18
  eliminating, 97
Agee, J., 82
Aguirre, J., 83
Ajayi, L., 34, 36n7, 81
Albers, P., 60
Aldana, U., 77
Allington, R. L., 32, 33n3, 35n4, 35n5, 36n6, 55
Altwerger, B., 10n5, 32
Alvarez, L., 22
Amanti, C., 10n4
American Association of Colleges for Teacher Education (AACTE), 91
American Educational Research Association (AERA), 2, 29, 37, 101, 102

American Psychological Association (APA), 2, 29, 37, 101, 102
Annual Measurable Achievement Objectives (AMAOs), 14, 21, 99
Annual Yearly Progress (AYP), 2
Antunez, B., 91
Applegate, A. V., 35n5, 36n6, 55
Applegate, V., 35n5, 36n6, 55
Arias, M. B., 91, 92
Artiles, A., 68, 102
Arya, P., 2, 10n5, 33, 36n7
Assaf, L., 18n3, 27, 27n4, 58
Assessment
  burden of, 13
  data provided by, instruction *vs.*, 33–34
  effects of, 13
  formative, 17–18
  of performance. *See* Performance assessments
  policy and practice changes in, 96–106
  of teacher candidates, 82–86
Ateh, C., 85
Atwell, N., 71
August, D., 2, 6n2, 10, 13n1, 18, 20, 29, 37, 75n9
Aukerman, M., 26, 35n5, 36n6, 59
Ávila, E., 66n6
Ávila, J., 36n7, 60, 94n7
AYP. *See* Annual Yearly Progress (AYP)

Bailey, A., 20, 69n7, 75, 100
Baker, E., 27, 86, 88, 89, 90, 90n5

Baker, K., 6
Bandeira de Mello, V., 68
Bandura, A., 28
Barboza, T., 86n4
Barton, P., 27, 86, 88, 89, 90, 90n5
Basal readers
  importance of, 58
  reading research and, 32–33
Bean, R., 5n1
Bean, T., 26
Beare, P., 83, 84
Beck, I., 5n1, 100
Benchmarking goals/practices
  ELLs experience with, 8–9, 10, 15
  in reading, 23–24
Berliner, D., 63, 77, 77n11, 96
Black, P., 17, 29
Black, R., 60
Blank, M., 77, 78
Blankenship, C., 68
Bloom, H. S., 5
Bomer, R., 10, 10n4
Borman, G. D., 32–33
Boulay, B., 5, 29
Boyd, M., 58n9
Bracey, G. W., 2, 27
Bransford, J., 91
Brill, M. T., 69, 72
Brock, L., 62
Brooks-Gunn, J., 63, 77n11
Brownell, M., 74
Brozo, W., 96
Buddin, R., 86, 87
Buese, D., 3, 10n5, 18n3, 27n4, 36n7, 39, 82
Bunch, G. C., 83
Butler, Y. G., 21, 61, 63, 74, 77, 102

California Alternate Performance
  Assessment (CAPA), 14
California Basic Educational Skills Test
  (CBEST), 83
California Commission on Teacher
  Credentialing, 92
California Department of Education
  (CDE), 4, 80, 103

California English Language
  Development Test (CELDT), 14,
  19–22, 24, 55, 62, 65, 101
California High School Exit Exam
  (CAHSEE), 14, 83
California Modified Assessment
  (CMA), 14
California Reading Initiative, 80
California Senate Bill 2042, 83–84
California Standards Test (CST), 8, 14,
  23, 67
  ELLs and, 1–2, 18–19
California State Assembly Bill 540, 65
California State Board of Education,
  4, 80
California Subject Examinations for
  Teacher (CSET), 83
California Teacher Performance
  Assessment (CalTPA), 84, 85, 92
Camarota, S., 63, 66
Campano, G., 60
Campbell, F. A., 77, 77n11
Capps, R., 66, 76, 77n12
Carey, J., 94
Carger, C. L., 63n4, 77n12
Carlisle, J., 5n1
Carlos (ELL student), case study, 64–66
Cazden, C., 37, 40
Chamberlain, A., 33
Chambers, B., 5, 33, 34, 100
Chambliss, M., 3, 10n5, 18n3, 27n4,
  36, 56, 82
Chavez, L., 76
Cheung, A., 5, 33, 100
Chiero, R., 84
Christian, D., 69n8
Chung, R. R., 83n2, 84, 84n3
Circle maps
  examples, 44f–48f
  problems with, 49–50
Classroom
  instructional practices and literacy
    events in, 37–56
  teacher-centered. *See* Teacher-
    centered classrooms
  testing-as-learning in, 27–28

Cohen, D., 88, 90
Cohn, D., 76
Coleman, R., 13n1, 29, 69n8, 101
Comber, B., 60
Conner, J. M., 32
Content
    sequence for teaching, testing and,
        79–80
    of teacher education programs, ELLs
        and, 103–105
    teaching and, 6
Contreras, F., 63, 65, 75n9, 77n12
Corn, J., 22
Cortina, K., 5n1
Costigan, A., 99n3
Cousin, P. T., 10n4
Crawford, J., 6
Croninger, R., 3, 10n5, 18n3, 27n4,
    82
Cross, C. T., 96
Cuban, L., 99n3
Cuéllar, D., 13, 63, 68, 75n9, 76
Cummins, J., 2, 20, 35n4
Curran, M., 92
Curriculum
    in California schools, 2, 4–11
    narrowing of, 27
    prepackaged. *See* Structured curricula
    program adoption in California, 4.
        See also Open Court *entries*

Damon, W., 80
Darling-Hammond, L., 27, 74, 83, 85,
    86, 88, 89, 90, 90n5, 91, 96, 104
Data
    assessment providing, instruction *vs.*,
        33–34
    on ELLs, disaggregation of, 101–102
    information *vs.*, 28
Davis, S., 5, 33
De Jong, E., 62n2, 69n8, 99, 104, 105
Delancy, D., 62
Delgado-Gaitan, C., 52
Denton, N. A., 63, 65
Díaz, E., 10n4
Diaz-Rico, L., 71

Dillon S., 68, 87
Disaggregation, of ELL data, 101–102
Dole, J., 5n1, 32, 36
Dooley, C. M., 27n4, 58, 98n2
Dowling, N. M., 32–33
Downey, M., 98
Draper, J., 5n1
Driscoll, A., 93
Dubin, J., 78
Duncan, A., 21, 90
Duncan, G., 63, 77n11
Dúran, R. P., 20, 74
Durkin, D., 56
Dutro, E., 38, 59
Dworin, J., 10, 10n4
Dyson, A. H., 35n5, 36n6, 53, 59, 106

Education Data Partnership, 14
Education policy
    assessment and instruction, changes
        in, 96–106
    and content, 103–5
    redesign attempts, 14
    research findings *vs.*, 24
    teacher performance assessments and,
        90
Education programs. *See* Teacher
    education programs
ELD. *See* English language development
    (ELD)
Elementary and Secondary Education
    Act (ESEA), xii, 97, 101, 102
Elementary schools. *See also* Laurel
    Elementary School
    accountability and surveillance in,
        14–17
Elementary Secondary Education Act
    (ESEA), 14, 77
Ellis, R., 75
ELLs. *See* English language learners
    (ELLs)
English language development (ELD)
    NCLB mandates and, 20–21
    providing opportunities for, 99–100
    restricted opportunities for, 57–58
    tests, 20

English language learners (ELLs),
    10–11
  assessment of, 10–11, 100–103
  benchmarking goals and, 8–9
  California Standards Test and, 1–2,
    18–19
  complexities of teaching, 62–78
  expanding literacy experiences for, 60
  helping, issues and recommendations
    for, 73–78
  identification of, 100–101
  policy changes in assessment of,
    100–103
  preparing teacher candidates to
    teach, 80–82
  setting goals for, 7–11
  "silent period" experience of, 8
  structure curricula for, making
    changes to, 59
  teacher education program content
    and, 103–105
  teaching of, 2, 6–11
  test accommodations for, 21, 103
  test score accuracy and, 35–36
  test texts, decoding problems with,
    22
  testing appropriately, 29, 102
  underachievement among, 6
  variety among (case studies), 61–73
Equal Educational Opportunities Act
    (EEOA), 68
Esra, P., 62
Estrada, P., 21, 61, 62, 65, 73, 75

Falk, B., 74
Fang, Z., 59, 94
Felch, J., 86, 90
Fessenden, F., 68
Fierros, E., 68
Fillmore, L. W., 91–92, 104
Financial savings, with reduced testing,
    97–98
Fix, M., 66, 76, 77n12
Fletcher, J. M., 33n2
Flores, B., 10n4
Folkes, A., 60

Foorman, B. R., 5n1, 33n2
Formative assessments, 17–18, 29–30, 94
Forum on Education Accountability, 96
*A Framework for Understanding
    Poverty* (Payne), 5
Francis, D. J., 21, 33n2
Franklin, R., 77
Frawley, W., 20
Freedson-Gonzalez, M., 91, 93, 105
Freire, P., 50, 56
Fresno Assessment of Student Teachers
    (FAST), 84
Frey, N., 29
Frontier, A., 13n2, 21, 27n4
Fry, R., 65
Fu, D., 59, 94
Fuchs, D., 34
Funding, 77
  for literacy coaches, 22
  for testing, 97–98
Furgiuele, C., 76, 77n12
Fusarelli, L., 74

Gabriel, T., 27
Gallimore, R., 66
Gallucci, C., 83
Gamoran, A., 59
Gamse, B. C., 5, 29
Gándara, P., 6n2, 20, 63, 65, 75n9, 76,
    77n12, 93, 103, 105
Garan, E., 35n4
García, E., 6, 13, 63, 68, 75n9, 76, 91,
    92, 93
García, G. E., 2, 13n1, 20, 29
Garnier, H., 66
Gates McGinitie test, 33
Gay, G., 10n4, 92
Genesee, F., 69n8
Genishi, C., 35n5, 36n6, 106
Gersten, R., 4, 33, 105
Geva, E., 20
Gibson, M. A., 76
Gilliland, B., 85
Goertz, M., 24
Goldenberg, C., 13n1, 29, 66, 69n8,
    99, 101

Gómez, M. C., 6n2, 75n9
Gonzáles, N., 10n4
Gonzales, R., 65, 66
Goodman, Y., 18, 29
Gorski, P., 10
Grady, K., 84–85
Graeber, A., 3, 10n5, 18n3, 27n4, 82
Graves, A., 29, 75
Greene, B. G., 32
Griffo, V., 36n7, 94n7
Grinberg, J., 91–92
Grodsky, E., 68
Grossman, P., 104
Guaglianone, C., 84
Gude, O., 60
Guévremont, A., 74
Gunderson, L., 34
Gutiérrez, K., 61n1

Haager, D., 34
Haberman, M., 10n4
Haertel, E., 27, 86, 88, 89, 90, 90n5
Hakuta, K., 21, 61, 63, 74, 77, 102
Haladyna, T. M., 103
Hamburger, L., 21, 61, 62, 65, 73, 75
Hammerness, K., 104
Harcourt Reading, 32
Harper, C., 62n2, 69n8, 99, 104, 105
Harrison, C., 17, 29
Harste, J. C., 60
Haskins, J., 39
Haskins, R., 77
Haxby, B., 34, 100
Hernandez, D. J., 63, 65, 77n12
Hernandez, S. H., 66, 76
Herrera, S., 60
Hiebert, E., 29, 33n3
Higareda, I., 68, 102
High-volume, high-stakes testing, 2–3, 13–30
    consequences of, 26–30
    preparing teachers for, 91–93
    shortcomings of, 96–97
Hill, M., 60
Ho, A. D., 2, 27
Hoffman, J., 18n3, 27

Home language Survey (HLS), 20, 69
Hondagneu-Sotelo, P., 65, 66n6
Hopkins, M., 6n2, 75n9
Horst, M., 5, 29
Hosp, J., 5n1
Hosp, M., 5n1
Houghton Mifflin, 4
*Houghton Mifflin Reading: A Legacy of
    Literacy* (Houghton Mifflin), 4, 32
Hudelson, S., 69n8
Hull, G., 60
Hunter, M., 5

Immigration issues, 65–66, 75–77
Independent reading, of stories, 50–53
Information, data *vs.*, 28
Insaurralde, A., 21, 61, 62, 65, 73, 75
Instruction
    effective, Hunter's essential elements
        of, 5
    policy and practice changes in,
        96–106
    in structured curriculum classroom,
        37–56
I-R-E prompts, 40, 57
Irvine, P., 38

Jacob, R. T., 5, 29
Jacobson, R., 77, 78
Jaeger, E., 36, 36n7
Janks, H., 60
Jin, L., 2, 10n5, 33, 36n7
Johnson, E., 34
Johnston, K., 32
José (ELL student), case study, 66–68

Kachur, R., 59
Kao, G., 13
Kato, A., 85
Kelly, K., 20, 69n7, 75, 100
Kemple, J., 5
Kerashen, S. D., 8
Kersten, J., 3, 36, 94
Kieffer, M., 21
Kim, J. S., 2
Kimball, S. M., 83

King-Jackson, V., 94
Kinsey, G., 84
Klingner, J., 34, 68
Knight, S., 93
Koda, K., 20
Koelsch, N., 21, 61, 62, 65, 73, 75
Kornfeld, J., 84–85
Koyama, J. P., 76
Kozol, J., 98n1
Krashen, S., 35n4, 35n5, 36n6
Ku, L., 76, 77n12

Labaree, D. F., 32n1
Ladd, H., 27, 86, 88, 89, 90, 90n5
Lagemann, E. C., 32n1
Lake, C., 5, 33
Lam, W. S. E., 60
Lamme, L. L., 59, 94
Land, R., 2, 56
Language
    parts of language, teaching of, 35
    of students in poverty, 10
    and testing, 1–12
Language arts standard, 24
Language proficiency
    achieving, 19–20
    measuring, 20–22
    NCLB mandates and, 20
Lantolf, J. P., 20
Larson, J., 38, 60
Laster, B., 2, 10n5, 33, 36n7
Laurel Elementary School
    classroom life in, 9–10
    neighborhood characteristics and,
        6–7
    prepackaged literacy curriculum in,
        problems and consequences,
        38–39
    reading benchmark tests in, 24
    student characteristics at, 6–7
    summative tests *vs.* formative
        assessments in, 18
    testing frequency at, 29
Lawton, T., 18n3, 28
Learning
    accountability and, 105–106

measuring student achievement.
    See Value-added measurement
    (VAM)
    and testing, reciprocity between,
        9–10
Learning goals
    evaluating, 1–3
    testing goals and, 7–8
Lee, C., 17, 29
Lee, S. K., 34, 36n7, 81
Lee, S., 62n2
Lefsky, E., 5n1
Lesaux, N., 20, 21
Limited English Proficient (LEP), 19–20
Lindholm-Leary, K., 69n8
Linn, R., 27, 86, 88, 89, 90, 90n5
Linquanti, R., 62
Linton, A., 77
Literacy coaches, funding for, 22
Literacy experiences
    expanding, research on, 60
    in structured curriculum classroom,
        37–56
Llosa, L., 17
Los Angeles Times, standardized test
    results analysis by, 86. *See also*
    Value-added measurement (VAM)
Losen, D., 6n2, 75n9
Lucas, T., 91–92, 93, 105
Ludovina, F., 76
Luke, A., 32

Macartney, S. E., 63, 65
Macy, S., 83, 84
Madaus, G., 17, 74, 81
Madden, N. A., 33, 34, 100
Marker, P., 84–85
Marshall, B., 17, 29
Marzano, R., 17, 94
Maxwell-Jolly, J., 93, 105
May, L., 10, 10n4
McCarthey, S., 53
McKenna, M., 34
McKnight, K. S., 60
McKnight, M. A., 34
McKoon, G., 2, 13n1, 20, 29

McLaughlin, D. H., 68
McNiven, S., 76, 77n12
McRae, D., 33
Medina, J., 27
Mehan, H., 37, 40
Mehta, P., 33n2
Mellard, D. F., 34
Menard-Warwick, J., 66
Menken, K., 18n3, 74, 75, 91
Mercado, D., 91–92, 93
Merickel, A., 62
Merit pay, value-added measurement
    and, 86–88
Miao, J., 17, 74, 81
Milanowski, A. T., 83
Milk, R., 91–92, 93
Miller-Johnson, S., 77, 77n11
Millman, J., 60
Modla, V., 35n5, 36n6, 55
Moll, L., 10n4
Monzó, L., 71
Morales, P. Z., 77
Morales-Ellis, L., 81n1, 82
Morrell, E., 60
Morse, S., 76
Mosely, M., 60
Moskin, M., 70
Moustafa, M., 2, 56
Munroe, K., 32
Murname, R., 88, 90
Murray, J., 66, 76, 77n12
Murri, N. H., 91, 92

Nagaoka, J., 74
Nation, I. S. P., 71
National Assessment of Educational
    Progress (NAEP), 18
National Center for Education Statistics
    (NCES), 14
National Council on Measurement in
    Education (NCME), 2, 29, 37,
    101, 102
The National Literacy Panel, 18
National Reading Panel (NRP), 32,
    35, 36
Nazario, S., 66n6, 76

NCLB. *See* No Child Left Behind
    (NCLB)
Nelson, K., 5n1
New teachers
    structured curricula and, 34
    testing mandates and, 79–95
Nichols, S., 50n8
Nicole (ELL student), case study,
    69–71
No Child Left Behind (NCLB), xi–xii,
    17–19, 39, 62, 68, 75, 77, 88,
    102
    assessment burdens and, 13
    and English language development
        (ELD) tests, 20–21
    language proficiency mandates, 20
    legacy of, 14
    tracking data under, 97
Nystrand, M., 59

Oakes, J., 37
Obama Administration, 14, 18
O'Brien, R., 42
Ogbu, J. U., 66
Okhremtchouk, I., 85
Oláh, L., 24
Olmedo, I., 66
Olneck, M. R., 66
Olsen, L., 62n2, 76
Open Court Reading, 2, 4–5, 10, 19,
    32, 34, 36, 39–43, 50
    classroom observations, 7–11
    positive results with, 5
    as prepackaged program example,
        31
    teacher-centered nature of, 10
    testing pressure and, 10
    Thinking Maps™ used in, 43–50
Open Court units, 7
    read aloud session beginning, 39–43
Orellana, M., 61n1
Orfield, G., 2
Organization for Economic
    Cooperation and Development, 96
Osborn, J., 32, 36
Ost, J., 66, 76, 77n12

Pacing
  in Open Court Reading program,
    2–3, 5, 7, 19, 38, 39, 42
  pressure imposed by, 99
  in teacher-centered classrooms, 57,
    58
Palmer, D., 6
Pardo, L., 3, 36, 94
Paris, S., 18n3, 27, 28, 55
Parks, R., 39
Parrish, T. B., 62
Passel, J., 66, 76, 77n12
Patterson, E., 18n3, 27
Paugh, P., 94
Payne, M., 84
Payne, R., 5, 10
Pearson, P. D., 32, 33n3, 34, 36n7,
    94n7
Pearson, S., 77, 78
Pease Alvarez, L., 36, 36n7, 81n1
Pecheone, R., 83n2, 84n3
Peck, C., 83
Pedulla, J., 17, 74, 81
Pennington, J., 82
Pérez, M., 62
Perez-Lopez, D., 76, 77n12
Performance Assessment of California
    Teachers (PACT), 83, 84, 85, 92
Performance assessments, 83–84
  future of, 85–86
  implementation of, 84–85
  value-added. *See* Value-added
    measurement (VAM)
Perlstein, L., 18n3
Perryman, J., 35
Petscher, Y., 5n1
Pheifer, D., 13n2, 21, 27n4
Policy. *See* Education policy
Popham, J., 17, 94
Portes, A., 75
Poverty
  impact of, 6–7, 77–78
  student language and, 10
Powers, D. L., 82
Prendergast, C., 59
Prepackaged curricula. *See* Structured

curricula
Pressley, M., 34
Previewing stories, Thinking Maps™
    and, 43–50
Progress in schools, public pressure for,
    15
Proposition 227, 6
Pungello, E., 77, 77n11

Quality, Adaptation, Incentive, and
    Time (QAIT) model, 33

Race to the Top Fund, 14
Ramchand, R., 76, 77n12
Ramey, C. T., 77, 77n11
Ramos, M., 17, 74, 81
Ranker, J., 60
Ravitch, D., 14, 27, 86, 88, 89, 90,
    90n5, 96, 97
Read aloud session, 39–43
Reading
  benchmarks for, 23–26
  research on, 32
  skills required for, 33
  of test texts, decoding problems,
    22–23
Reading Benchmark progress chart, 16
Reading First, 4–5
  funding for testing and, 97–98
  literacy coaches funded by, 7
Reading First Skills Assessments, 15,
    16, 23
  class discussion about, 24–26
  decoding problems in, 22–23
  reading benchmarks and, 29
  tracking scores from, 22
  unit tests, 22–23
Reading Instruction Competence
    Assessment, 80–81
Reading lessons
  independent reading, 50–53
  previewing a story, 43–50, 44f–48f
  read aloud session in, 39–43
Reciprocity, between learning and
    testing, 9–10
Reese, L., 66, 75n9

Research
  on expanding literacy experiences, 60
  on reading, 32
Richards, R., 34, 36n7, 81
Riggan, M., 24
Rinke, C., 80
Rivera, M., 21
Roderick, M. R., 74
Rogers, R., 60
Roos, N., 74
Rose Report, 35
Roth, J., 18n3, 28
Rothstein, R., 27, 86, 88, 89, 90, 90n5
Rouse, C., 77
Rubin, D., 58n9
Ruddell, M., 84–85
Rueda, R., 68, 71, 102
Ruiz, N., 81n1, 82
Rujumba, K., 86
Rumbaut, R., 75
Russell, M., 17, 74, 81
Russell, S., 94
Rust, F., 104

Sahni, U., 60
Sakurai, G., 43
Salas, R., 18n3, 27
Salazar, J., 68, 102
Salomone, R., 76
Samuels, S. J., 35n5, 36n6
Samway, K. D., 29, 36, 36n7, 69, 71,
  81n1
Sapiens, A., 91–92, 93
Saunders, W., 69n8
Schatschneider, C., 33n2
Schemo, D., 68
Schmida, M., 21, 61, 62, 65, 73, 75
Schneck, C., 32–33
Scholarly traits, 10
School neighborhood, impact of
  poverty on, 6–7
Schools
  elementary, accountability and
    surveillance in, 14–17. *See also*
    Laurel Elementary School
  progress in, public pressure and, 15

Scientifically based research (SBR), 32
  accuracy of, 35–36
  parts of language and, 35
  problems with, 36–37
Second language acquisition. *see*
  English language learners (ELLs)
Seiki, S., 85
Semingson, P., 10, 10n4
Serna, C., 91, 92
Shanahan, T., 10, 13n1, 18, 20, 29, 37,
  100
Shannon, P., 32
Shavelson, R., 27, 86, 88, 89, 90, 90n5
Shelton, N., 36, 36n7
Shepard, L., 27, 86, 88, 89, 90, 90n5
Shiel, G., 96
Shin, F., 23
Short, D., 69n8
Shulman, L., 104
Siegel, L., 20
"Silent period," in ELL experience, 8
Single Subject Assessments for Teaching
  (SSAT), 83
Skills assessment tests. *See* Reading
  First Skills Assessments
Skindrud, K., 4, 33
Slavin, R. E., 34, 100
Slavin, R., 5, 33, 100
Sloan, T., 83
Smith, D., 86, 90
Smith, J. R., 63, 77n11
Smith, K., 60
Snow, C., 91–92, 104
Snyder, J., 80, 83
Socias, M., 62
Socioeconomic status, 63, 68, 77–78
Solórzano, R., 20, 21
Song, J., 86, 90
Spain, A., 62
Sparling, J., 77, 77n11
Special Education Reading Task Force,
  80
Speroni, C., 62
SRA/McGraw-Hill, 2, 4, 34, 40, 41,
  42, 43. *See also* Open Court
  Reading

Stamina writing exercises
  described, 54
  examples of, 54–55
  purpose of, 55–56
Standardized tests
  described, 17
  effects of, 17–24
  overuse of, 17
  results analysis by *Los Angeles
    Times*, 86. *See also* Value-added
    measurement (VAM)
Standards for Education and
  Psychological Testing, 18–19
Stansbury, K., 83n2
Stevens, L. P., 26
Stories
  independent reading of, 50–53
  previewing with Thinking Maps™,
    43–50
Stornaiuolo, P., 60
Stritikus, T., 6n3, 93
Structured curricula, 31–60
  alternatives to, 34
  appeal of, 31–34
  consequences of, 56–57
  effects on teaching practices, 36
  limitations of, 37–56
  modification of, 39
  monitoring of, 38
  problems with, 34–37, 81
  scientific approach to, 32–34
  success of, 34
  suggested changes to, 58–60
  teacher education and, 94–95
Students. *See also* English language
    learners (ELLs)
  accountability pressures on, 20
  measuring learning level of. *See*
    Value-added measurement
    (VAM)
  sharing test scores with, 15–17
Styles, M., 35n4
Suárez-Orozco, C., 65, 75n9, 76,
    76n10, 77
Suárez-Orozco, M., 65, 75n9, 76,
    76n10, 77

Success for All (reading reform
    program), 33
Sullivan, A., 68
Summative tests, 17
Sunderman, G., 2
Support, for teachers, 93–94
Surveillance, in elementary schools,
    14–16
  effects of, 16–17
Swartz, J., 32
Sweeney, J., 63

Takanishi, R., 77
Tanner, D., 83, 84
Tara (student), case study, 71–73
Taumlinson-Clarke, S., 92
Taylor, D., 69, 71
Teacher candidates
  assessment of, 82–86
  preparation for teaching ELLs, 80–82
Teacher education programs, 104
  in accountability context, 94–95
  changes in, 104
  ELLs and, 103–105
  enhancements to, 104–105
Teacher Performance Assessment (TPA),
    83–86, 92
Teacher-centered classrooms, 57
  high-volume, high-stakes testing
    experience and, 10, 17
  pacing requirement in, 57, 58
  strategies for making changes to, 59
Teacher/teachers
  education and support of, 91–94,
    104–105
  enhancing knowledge of, 104–105
  measuring effectiveness of. *See* Value-
    added measurement (VAM)
  as "primary knower," 59
  training *vs.* educating, 82
Teaching
  common approach to, implementing, 5
  and content, 6
  of English Language Learners, 2,
    6–12
  methods of, 27

of parts of language, 35
preparation for, 80–82
reductive approach to language arts, 56–57
with structured curricula, strategies for changes to, 58–60
test-oriented, 27, 96–97
Téllez, K., 83, 92, 105
Teresa (ELL student), case study, 62–64
Test scores, 24, 102
accuracy of, 35–36
as cause of low self-esteem, 16–17, 28
and data, 28
effects of, 86–87
importance of, 2–3
public reporting of, 15–17
Testing-as-learning, 27–28
Testing/tests. *See also* Reading First Skills Assessment
alternatives to, 30
California standard, 18–22
class discussions about, 24–26
content sequence for, 79–80
in elementary schools, 13–30
of ELLs, 74–75
financial burden of, 97–98
Gates McGinitie, 33
high-volume, high-stakes. *See* High-volume, high-stakes testing
impact on teacher, 17
and language, 1–12
learning and, reciprocity between, 9–10
standardized, 17–24. *See also* Standardized tests
time burden of, 98–100
Test-oriented teaching, 27, 96–97
Texas Assessment of Academic Skills (TAAS), 82
Texas Assessment of Knowledge and Skills (TAKS), 82
Thinking Maps™, 43–50, 59
circle map examples, 44f–48f
mandated use of, 5
problems with, 49–50
Thinking Maps Inc, 69, 72

Tienda, M., 13
Time issues
ELLs and, 73–74
reduced testing and, 98–100
teaching content and, 79–80
Toch, T., 17, 97
Todorova, I., 75n9, 76
Topping, K., 96
Torgerson, C., 83, 84
Toste, J., 5n1
Turner, G., 5n1
Turner, J., 18n3, 28
Turque, B., 89
Tyack, D., 76

Underachievement, among ELLs, 6
Underwood, C., 60
Unlu, F., 5, 29
Urbina, I., 68
Uriarte, M., 6n2, 75n9
U.S. Department of Education, 14, 18

Valdés, G., 13, 66, 75n9, 76
Valenzuela, A., 73, 75n9, 76
Valli, L., 3, 10n5, 18n3, 27n4, 36, 36n7, 39, 56, 80, 82
Value-added measurement (VAM)
cautionary considerations, 88–90
merit pay and, 86–88
pressures associated with, 94–95
Vasudevan, L., 60
Vaughn, S., 34
Villegas, A. M., 91, 93, 105
Vinovskis, M., 14, 96
Vogt, M. E., 69n8
Vygotskty, L., 59

Wallace, M., 85
Walpole, S., 34
Walqui, A., 21, 61, 62, 65, 73, 75
Warchauer, M., 60
Ware, P. D., 60
Warren, J. R., 68
Waxman, H., 92, 105
Weed, K., 71
Weinstein, C., 92

Weinstein, R., 28, 37, 62n3
Weiss, S., 21, 61, 62, 65, 73, 75
Welner, K., 68
*What Teacher's Need to Know About
    Language* (Snow & Fillmore),
    104–105
White, B., 83
Wiley, T., 6n2
William, D., 17
William, W., 17, 29
Wilson, G. P., 10n5
Wiltz, N., 10n5
Wiseman, D., 93
Witt, D., 21, 61, 63, 74, 77, 102
Woodbridge, S., 60
Working Group on ELL Policy, 62
Wright, W., 6n2, 6n3, 13n2, 18n3, 21,
    68, 74, 81, 99

Writing
    opportunities for, 53–56
    proficiency in, 1–2
Wyse, D., 35n4

Xu, S. H., 69n8

Yatvin, J., 35n4
Yeung, J. W., 63, 77n11

Zacher Pandya, J., 36n7, 54, 60, 90n6,
    94n7
Zavis, A., 86n4
Zellmer, M., 13n2, 21, 27n4
Zeng, J., 5n1
Zigmond, N., 5n1
Zimmerman, J., 4, 32n1
Zlolniski, C., 65n5

About the Author

Jessica Zacher Pandya is an Associate Professor in the Departments of Teacher Education and Liberal Studies at California State University, Long Beach. She engages in ethnographic research to understand children and youths' literacy practices in context. She has written extensively about children's identity work in elementary classrooms, and has published in journals such as *Research in the Teaching of English*, *Language Arts*, and *Educational Studies*.